IN LOVE AND WAR

Finding the father I neglected to know

ANDREW BETHELL

Copyright © 2025 Andrew Bethell

Published by Tricorner Press.

All rights reserved

No part of this book may be reproduced in any form or by any electronic or mechanical means, including in information storage and retrieval systems, without permission in writing from the author.

The author has asserted their right under the Copyright, Designs and Patents Act 1988 to be identified as the author of this work.

Paperback ISBN: 978-1-8383315-3-5

For Katherine, Matthew and Ben and their children, and children's children.

In memory of Claire.

Memory and forgetting: these are the faculties of mind by which we are aware of time, and time is a mystery. In addition, a long tradition holds that the imagination is best conceived as operating with a mixture of memory and forgetting. Creation—things coming into being that never were before—that too is a mystery.
Lewis, Hyde. A Primer for Forgetting.

I told her how, a few days earlier, I'd run to catch an elevator in the Kremlin and suddenly seen my face in the mirror. Only it wasn't me staring back from the elevator wall, it was my father. He'd appeared unexpectedly, but he now dogged my steps. I saw him every morning while shaving; he looked at me with surprise and a touch of irony. My father's face, which I'd come to inhabit despite my many efforts to avoid it. And the skull behind it, now clearly coming into view, awaiting its hour, etching its imprint on my features, as they became ever more drawn.
Giuliano de Empoli, The Wizard of the Kremlin

Contents

Chapter 1: The Father Speaks 1
Chapter 2: Dunkirk 11
Chapter 3: An Unexpected Graveyard 25
Chapter 4: A Ghost-Written Autobiography 41
Chapter 5: A Death on the Rock 47
Chapter 6: A Normal School Holiday Morning 49
Chapter 7: The Coroner's Inquest 65
Chapter 8: The Funeral 69
Chapter 9: Back to School 77
Chapter 10: School Fees 81
Chapter 11: School Fragments 89
Chapter 12: Captured on Recce Ridge 103
Chapter 13: Mrs Bethell waits for news 115
Chapter 14: Drew's story with scenes from the film 125
Chapter 15: The Anzio Beach Head 147
Chapter 16: Breaking the Gothic Line 173
Chapter 17: Pam's Story 195
Chapter 18: Falling in love 215
Chapter 19: Getting to Know You 227
Chapter 20: The Palestine Question 251
Chapter 21: Proposal, Marriage and Me 267
Obituary 297
Sources 302
Acknowledgements 304
About the Author 305

CHAPTER 1

The Father Speaks

Nocera Umbria, Tuscany. 17th October 1987

In 1987 I was lucky enough to make a film about my father. He and many thousands of allied prisoners of war were released in 1943, when the Italian forces surrendered and ceased to take responsibility for securing the prisoner of war camps. He was aged twenty-two and he walked over 450 miles down the spine of Italy to reach the Allied lines. It was an act of bravery and as I found out more about his exploits, it showed me so many of the qualities that made him a remarkable man through to his death at the untimely age of sixty-seven. Although, when he eventually told me about his exploits, I was not a professional film maker, I managed to raise the money to make the film. Together we retraced his route and found many of the people who had helped him on his journey. He died just three months after we completed filming.

While making that film with him I was able to observe, up close, the qualities that had sustained him through his long walk and were equally on show in the film, and indeed in the making of the film. He was able to mix determination with charm, guile with sincerity and generosity with good will. He was an enthusiast, outgoing and socially adept. He was open to whatever the world would throw at him and grasped the opportunities he had in his life with passion and flair. He was my father and I was proud of him. But I never really got to know him. He was from the generation which believed that emotions however strongly felt should be restrained even within the intimacy of his family.

We will get on to the film and the story of his escape later in this book, but there is one scene from the film, that sticks in my mind and the minds of most who have watched it. In fact, it is the scene that triggered my efforts to re-discover my father, so it is right that it should begin the journey of this book.

1987

Interior

Pizza Restaurant, Norcera Umbria.
Evening. The plates are clean and the carafe of wine is almost empty. Andrew and his father Drew are discussing the days filming. After more wine the conversation takes an unexpected turn.

Andrew: I'm conscious of the fact that this trip was the first time that we have had unadulterated contact with each other for now for two weeks getting on for three . .

Drew: *(Lighting his cigarette in its black holder)* Numbing isn't it?

(Uneasy laughter)

Andrew: *(Flustered)* Well it may be numbing but it doesn't half tell you about yourself. I feel that I'm getting to know you in a way, that honestly for forty years, I haven't. Do you feel you're getting to know me in a way that you haven't?

Extended pause and a long drag of his cigarette via its holder.

Drew: Mmmm. . . . .(slow intake of breath). . . um... . .. Nnn . . .not really.

Andrew subsides as the full impact of this rejection sinks in. He needs to step back and try another tack.

Andrew: Well for example, it took you fifty years to tell me the story of this escape and I am wondering why you didn't tell me more? Earlier.

Drew: Ummm . . . I find that almost impossible to explain. I think you have to go back to, where are we now, 1987, you have to go back to the sixties and think what the climate was then. Certainly, talking about the last war was not ….um. . . a very interesting subject to anybody. It was all deadbeat stuff.

Andrew: Ahh.

Drew: I suppose you could say, one was brought up not to talk about <u>you</u>.

Andrew: *(Surprised)* Not to talk about <u>me</u>?

Drew: No, <u>me</u>.

Andrew: Oh <u>you</u>! I understand. Not to talk about 'oneself'.

Drew: Yes, brought up not to talk about <u>oneself</u>.

A moment of the purest clarity. A self-evident truth that spoke for his generation. A generation that found it difficult to use the first person. So much safer to say 'oneself' rather than 'myself'. The disconnected third person was a place of safety for men who had been brought up to avoid raw emotion. It was a defence against the emotional vulnerabilities that might otherwise spill out. I, on the other hand, believed that I came from that post-war generation that felt at ease with the first person.

That was a conversation with my father that did happen. It is my father's authentic voice. Not quite the last conversation we ever had before his death, but the last attempt to address our relationship and his relationship to the past.

Apart from that brief interchange in the pizza restaurant in Norcera, I failed to engage with my father on any other level than the pragmatic, the functional, the here and now. We spoke about his job, about my job and about his hobbies. He opened up briefly, in his moment of grief at my brother's suicide, but quickly closed that conversation down in the interests of emotional preservation. That solitary moment recorded on film where I risk trying to build some sort of bridge over which we could explore our relationship and was cruelly denied, must be the exception that proves the rule.

It is now thirty-six years since his death and listening to that extract from the film was what prompted me to try and reconstruct the man I neglected to know. In particular, I realise that I knew so little about the rest of his war, the part he never shared with me. I may know the story of his escape but so much else about what happened to him on the beaches of Dunkirk, the sands of North Africa and the arduous battle for Italy is a blank. I know the bare bones but none of the detail. And I was sadly ignorant about what happened to him in the two years after the war. These are very significant years for me. It was just after the war that he met my mother and then courted her for two years by letter. I was lucky enough to find the letters he wrote during that period and though them I can construct how this surprising passion and love eventually resulted in his marriage and my conception. So, this is a book about love and war.

In order to reconstruct so much of what happened during my father's war I have had to rely on my imagination. As they say in the drama documentaries:

Based on the truth but where there is no record, recreated based on the best available evidence.

There are some facts, some archive, a few second-hand recollections all mixed up with a great deal of imagination. It's the best I can do. Perhaps it will help me to understand the father I never really got to know. I am trying to make sense of his legacy. As I now exceed his life span by ten years, I sense a growing affinity with the man. I am growing old as he grew old and progressively discovering how we reproduce more than we transform. I am my father's son. It cannot be denied. I see his face in the mirror.

Of course, I cannot recreate the conversations that we never had, and anyway they are bound to be false narratives as I have no indication that he would have lost any of the deep reticence he displayed in the pizza restaurant. Instead, I will write him some letters in which I will share with his ghost some retrospective insights, as well as my admiration, even my love.

Stoke Newington, London January 2024

Dear Dad,

When you died, in the Spanish port of Calpe, on your 67th birthday, I flew out to support my mother. An unexpected heart attack that killed you off in the time it took your wife to go downstairs to make you a birthday cup of tea. It was a shock, of course. But as so often happens the focus is on the living and then on the logistics. What's to be done in a foreign land? You would have been very good at that. You loved getting things done and your rudimentary Spanish would have stood us in good stead. But you were gone, so it was left to us. Arrangements to be made in a bureaucracy of death management even more alienating than our own.

It was a system that meant you were laid out in your coffin with the lid off in the local cemetery prior to your cremation and I was allowed to go and see you. It was our last encounter and I wept in a way that you might have found embarrassing. I was weeping for the loss of you, of course, but much more for the loss of opportunity. I wept for what we hadn't done or said, and, more starkly, for what we might have done and said. I was berating myself for my failure to make more effort to understand you and your life. I realised that even though I had done so much more than most, by setting up and making a film about your wartime escape, I still didn't know you and there were so many things that I wanted to know: much of what else happened to you in the war that never got talked about

I am going to try to catch up. A bit late in the day and most of the people who could have given me answers to the many questions, added colour to the story, are now dead. I let them go too. So, what am I left with? Well, the answer is 'not much'. Our family are not great archivists so there is little hard paper evidence (the exception being the treasure trove of love letters you wrote to my mother). So, although I am not sure you would approve, I am going to grasp the splinters of hard fact that linger in formal archives, delve for the likely apocryphal anecdotes that did get passed down and mix it all up with a large chunk of my own imagination. It will, of necessity, be a partial and episodic account. I will go back to your origins, your childhood, your school days and the catastrophe that took your father. After that I am going to restrict myself to your war and the immediate aftermath. Once the war is over, I will enjoy trawling through your love letters to understand how and why you fell in love with my mother. And since I was born in 1947 a year after you married her, that will be my end stop. I like to think I will stop telling your story at the moment I entered the picture. What the Freudians call 'the primal scene'.

I also need to warn you that I plan to participate in the scenes that I conjure up using the clues that I have and my powers of imagination. I want to be there. I want, as much as possible, to feel what you felt. I will be there but not there. I will be the time traveller: a passive observer not a participant. I will be watching as you experience the traumatic moments of your young life. You could call me a trauma tourist.

I am going to start on the beaches of Dunkirk. Although you were happy to share your wartime escape with me (and others on the BBC), you never said a word about what happened when you joined the army and arrived in France on your 19th birthday. So, I am going to have to make it up.

With love

Hum,

PS. It was only after you died that mum explained why you called me Hum throughout my life. Apparently when I was a baby your nickname for me was 'Humblezoomer', later shortened to Hum. Strange that I never sought to understand it until long after you had gone.

CHAPTER 2

Dunkirk

Bray Dunes Plage. May 27th, 1940

It is dawn. I am in the beach at *Bray-Dunes Plage*, some two miles east of Dunkirk. It is a grey dirty day. No sign of spring. The air is acrid. We are down wind of the town of Dunkirk where the oil storage tanks have been burning for days.

A track has been cut through the dunes and to my right there's a collection of vehicles. Mostly abandoned, like the men who drive them, stuck in the sand with nowhere else to go. I watch groups of men beginning to wake. There is an air of resigned lethargy. These men are exhausted. Their clothes are muddy and their eyes are hollow. Vacant. One man has three stripes on the sleeve of his grubby tunic, but he too is moving slowly. He has little to say, no commands to give. His status seems to have drained away into the sand. The role of sergeant relies on orders from above, on an objective, on a need to get things done. Right now, there is little to do. In as much as there is a plan, nobody has told this sergeant so he has nothing to tell his men. His unit has played its part in the rear-guard action that held back the *blitzkrieg* for a few days and nights. But they had merely delayed the inevitable His unit had helped make an almost impossible rescue possible. But now he and his men are in a state of stasis. They are waiting.

In front of me is a lorry, a Bedford 3 tonner. It looks robust with a chunky cabin section and what I now know is the emblem of the 1st Division of the British Expeditionary Force painted onto the nearside bumper. Its heavy-duty tyres have spun themselves deep into the sand. The camouflaged canopy is torn and flaps in the light wind. This lorry has come to the end of its tour.

I am staring at the figure in the passenger seat. He is asleep, his inert face squashed against the glass, distorting what I know to be his handsome youthful features. I cannot see, but it is easy to imagine the trail of deep sleep dribble that has escaped his mouth and run down his unshaven chin. He hasn't shaved for five days but his stubble is soft because this man is young. This is the fresh face of youth undone by a premature exposure to the worst a war can dish out. His hair is greasy but slicked back in the style of the times. He comes from an age when young men were quick to take on the style of their elders. On his shoulder I can see a single pip. He is a second lieutenant He joined his regiment, the 19th Field Regiment, Royal Artillery as soon as he graduated from the Officer Training Corps in January 1940. He has been in charge of the men who are slowly coming to in the sand around his vehicle, for only a few short weeks. Most are older with darker bristles on their chin. They are used to having their destiny controlled by fresh faced youths of the officer class. They bear no grudges. They accept that he is up there in the cab and they are sleeping on the sand. They know it is the sergeant, not the young man in the cab, who delivered the orders that have got them here.

The second lieutenant sleeps on. Dreaming of a different, safer place perhaps.

Were he to wake, his elevated position would give him a good view out to sea, where ships of the British navy are waiting in the distance, half hidden in the mist and smoky haze. Frigates, Destroyers. Corvettes all with many feet of draught that keep them far off the beach. They have come as far as they can. The troops who wait and watch in precarious expectation will soon begin to see a flock of smaller boats, the famous little ships, that may be able to get them off the beach and out to the safety of a deep draught ship.

The men around the Bedford 3 tonner are now awake. The simple solitary acts of waking have been replaced with the cold, miserable reality. The brutal truth is etched on their faces: we lost, we were routed, humiliated. Who will come to rescue this defeated rabble? Do we deserve to be saved?

Protected from the sounds of his men and their inescapable sense of failure, the second lieutenant sleeps on. He does not hear the distant sound of planes *en route*. The Luftwaffe have a schedule for their raids on these undefended losers. Seven am, two pm and just before dusk at six pm. I turn towards the distant drone and I am just in time to watch the flock of Heinkel bombers cruise towards the town of Dunkirk some two miles down the beach. They emerge through the plumes smoke that have been hanging in the air ever since the oil tanks on the outskirts were bombed three days ago. I am mesmerised by how the bombs land. First the shock waves, then the spurt of dust and rubble and then several seconds later, the sound arrives: a sharp crump. At this distance it is hard to feel the shock and awe. But I know that in the harbour thousands of men have been waiting on the mole, the fractured harbour wall where they wait patiently for rescue, and they will be watching the bombs descend: onto them and the ships that might have saved them.

Now, I am listening for another sound, because I am visiting from the future and know what will happen next. I have heard the story, if only the bare bones, I know enough to recognise the sound I am hearing now. It is the sound that really matters for the young man asleep in the passenger seat of the Bedford 3-tonner above *Bray-Dune Plage* just after dawn on the 28th May 1940.

He has not moved. His face is still pressed against the glass, misshapen by the vacancy of sleep. I, on the other hand am wide awake and I can hear the predatory howl of other planes approaching from the west. Unseen but imminent. A flock of raptors on its way. I know that sound, I have heard it in the grainy newsreels. It is the sound of Stukas. The Junker 87 or *Sturzkampfflugzeug,* the German dive bomber equipped 'with a propeller driven siren, known as "Jericho Trumpet", fitted on each undercarriage leg for the purpose of 'damaging enemy morale and causing physiological damage.'

I am focused on one plane in particular because it has broken from the group. It has spotted a likely cluster of troops, crouching in the sand and scrabbling for some cover whilst simultaneously jamming on their helmets in anticipation. Any cover will do. Spreading out, anything to increase the chances of survival. Some run for the ruined block house but their feet are sucked into the sand and they stumble. One or two roll under an abandoned half-track partly destroyed by a previous bomb.

I am not concerned with those others. They are awake and can take some sort of action to protect themselves. I am focused on one particular Stuka which I can see clearly now. I see its kinked wings black against the lightening sky. It has started to dive. The Jericho Trumpets have started to howl. Hard, metallic dissonance. Louder and louder. It assaults the ear drums. Invades the soul, just as intended.

I need to slow things down. Slow motion. A trick of my trade. Multiply the frames per second. But you cannot slow down sound. It distorts, denying the acoustic horror. The animal yowl is reaching a crescendo.

And now, at last, the second lieutenant hears it too and has jerked awake. For a brief moment the depth of his sleep and the containment of the cab has protected him from the aural onslaught.

I am watching him closely – closely observing my 19-year-old father a fraction of a second before his nemesis. An elongated moment in time- his time, not mine.

The Stuka finally pulls out of its screaming dive. The sound changes as it pulls away towards the beach. There is a new sound: the syncopated rattle of machine gun fire as it rakes the line of waiting men who look up and duck and dive to flatten themselves in the wet sand, as if that will make any difference to their chances.

I have no time for them, I am gripped by the sight of the single bomb that was released as the dive had reached its vertex. I am still in slo-mo: a thousand frames per second gives me plenty of time to follow the bomb's trajectory which leads inexorably towards the Bedford 3-tonner.

The second lieutenant knows none of this, he is just relieved to see the plane head off towards the beach. He assumes a reprieve. He may even be wiping the sleep from his eyes. I, on the other hand, know that we have reached a moment that statisticians would call the 'random variable': the point in time and space when the range of outcomes cannot be predicted. This is chaos theory: when kinetic energy, deviation and atmospheric fluctuation can each play a singular role in the final destination of this bomb. A tiny fraction of a degree will make all the difference. From where I sit the bomb is heading for the cab, the business end. Heading for my father. As it stands the odds are looking bad. It looks as if the bomb will destroy the engine, the seats, the dashboard, the steering wheel and my nineteen-year-old father. And by extension, me.

But then, and now I must slow the scene down into individual frames so that I can scrutinise this critical moment of deviation, I see the bomb drop from its glide path. Gravity has taken it

1940

from its preordained destination. The cab is spared. Instead, it rips through the canopy and smashes into the flat bed of the truck and detonates its twenty kilograms of high explosive. My father will not die today.

I am relieved. But then, of course, I knew that he would survive. He cannot die here on the beach at Bray-Dunes aged nineteen years at the very start of his army career. I need him to endure. He needs to procreate. My seventy-five years of life required the bomb to respond to a random gravitational tweak and hit the back of the truck not my father. Had the random variable delivered another outcome, I too would have been done for. For that relief much thanks.

I am only allowed that reprieve for a few more micro seconds, because you cannot bomb the back of a truck without catastrophic repercussions for whoever is in the front. After the explosion the base appears to flatten as the cab rears up into the air, like some ghastly prehistoric monster screaming in agony. It seems to hang in the air for another elongated moment giving me just enough time to feel the terrified anticipation for what comes next. Then it crashes back to earth with a fractured clang as the front axle snaps in two and the windscreen shatters.

I see the marionette-like figure of my father at first thrown back as the cab rears up and his head is smashed against the roof. Then, as it hits the ground again, this jangled puppet man is thrown forward and his head smashes into the dashboard. I can feel the impact as frame by frame his face hits the unyielding metal surface. No air bags here or the soft plastic cladding of modern vehicles, just the utilitarian brutal metal surface that crushes his mouth but spares his nose. Before the full force of the impact can deliver its aftershock, I note his slicked-back hair has escaped and is wild and loose. His trajectory has come to an abrupt halt. His head is resting now. I see no blood. Perhaps he sleeps.

The sergeant is the first to arrive. At first the door will not open. He calls for help and another gunner goes to the tool box lodged in what remains of the chassis. He finds a metal bar and together they prise open the door. My father does not move. But now I see the blood, it is pouring from his mouth. And, had I been able to go closer and look over the sergeant's shoulder I would have seen, in amongst the blood and spit dripping onto the floor of the cab, his teeth scattered on the muddy foot plate. I would have expected to see teeth, because I know that for the next fifty-two years of his life he wore false teeth. I have always assumed he lost his teeth on the beach at Dunkirk. He never told me how but his medical records confirm my supposition.

The sergeant calls for the field doctor. The cry is passed down the line. No one knows whether there is a doctor nearby. The few doctors and medical orderlies who made it to the beach are otherwise engaged. Overwhelmed with the wounded: shot up, blown up, decimated. Tens of thousands: a dejected and defeated army waiting for an unlikely rescue exposed and vulnerable. Mere flesh and bone against the persistent onslaught from the air, each one resulting in yet more wounded and many beyond helping. The few medics that were on the beach that day were not available to treat the second lieutenant.

1940

No doctor came but a bombardier brings an inadequate battle scarred first aid pack. The sergeant and three others gently extract my father from the cab, lowering him to the sand as one cautiously tries to remove the glass fragments from his neck and hands. They lay him out on the sand. He is out cold. Not only did his face crunch against the dash board, but his head had cracked against the roof of the cabin. The sergeant does his best to find his pulse. He fails, like all amateurs, he knows it is harder than it looks. (As I watch, I feel for my own pulse and fail to find it. But I am alive so he must be. I reassure myself). The pulse fails to reveal itself but there is breathe. I can see that. The blood bubbles out of his mouth. He is breathing. My father is alive.

The sergeant dabs at the bloody gash with a dressing. There is blood too on the back of his head. They start to bandage his head. There is some debate as to whether they should cover his mouth. He will need to eat and drink. They compromise and stuff a dressing into his mouth. It soon turns red.

I am touched by the way these battle-weary men who could so easily have been scornful of the sad spectacle of a smooth skinned public-school boy, minister to his wounds. They care for him. But their ministrations are interrupted by another Stuka attack. This time three machines flying up the beach seeking out the men sheltering in the dunes. They are flying low and I see flashes from the two 7.92 mm MG 17 machine guns set back in the wings: two hundred rounds per second. There is nowhere to hide. A stream of bullets lacerates the sand, and men cry out as hot metal enters flesh and splinters bones. One Stuka drops a bomb which explodes next to a lone ambulance abandoned on the beach. There are men crouched around it hoping to benefit from the misplaced assumption that the red cross stencil on its tattered canopy will somehow elicit mercy from the *Flugzeugführer* who has, it transpires, no time for convention. The spurt of sand hides the impact of his bullets. It is hard, from this distance, to appreciate the degree of carnage.

The strafing, raking staccato gunfire rips up the dunes towards my father and his men. A minor miracle causes the firing to stop some twenty yards back and the plane veers left out over the beach where there is even less shelter and the pickings are even easier. The lines of men collapse like wheat to the aerial scythe. Then those who can, scramble back onto their feet determined not to lose their places in the queue. The Stuka heads out to sea which is now dotted with small boats, some in the shallows with men desperately scrambling over the side. It zeros in on a pleasure steamer from leafy Marlow and drops its bomb onto the crowded deck, then spirals up and away as bodies burn and what is left begins to sink into the oily swell. Easy pickings.

Half an hour after the explosion, the second lieutenant, my father, is still comatose but there are signs of life. The sergeant has found his pulse and his head is moving as the pain meets his sluggish dawning consciousness. Some hours later an RAMC orderly arrives with a stretcher and a more reassuring knapsack of medical supplies. They move him into the partial protection of the ruined block house and the medic slips him some morphine. He sleeps.

It is time for me to leave the scene of battle. I am an interloper, a trauma tourist. Of course, my so-called observation is a complete fiction. I have an idea what the beach must have looked like from photos and filmed reconstructions, but when it comes to what it must have *felt* like to be there, I am lacking even the most basic information. I have described what probably happened to my father aged nineteen, but all I have to go by when it comes to feeling what he felt is to try and put myself in the same position. But, it's too late for that too. It will be a sham. And yet I want to try.

He was a product of his time. As we will see, he had had a 1930s training in trauma management. It's called a public-school education. I too had a public-school education, at the same school even, but by the time I was nineteen I was a child of the sixties. I can muse on what it might have felt like to have been sent into battle just at the moment when all vestige of imperial self-confidence would be shattered. I try to imagine what it felt like to be part of the British Expeditionary Force that was about to be put to the sword and then run for its life.

He had been subject to a rudimentary training when he joined his regiment, He was put in charge of a troop of thirty gunners with one sergeant and a bombardier, both of whom would have years more experience. I took on my first job as a teacher aged twenty and I was in charge of thirty young people, but nothing in my life then or indeed since provides even a hint as to what it must have felt like to be on the receiving end of constant attack on the ground and in the air from the well trained and ruthless Wehrmacht storming through Belgium.

The entire British army was in desperate retreat and despite the courage and the cussed determination, defeat was always inevitable. This was a beaten army and my father had joined up full of positivity, hoping to fight for King and Country, just as his army was found wanting. Underprepared and under equipped.

He will stay on the beach for five long days. His troop is waiting for the rest of the regiment which, as part of 1st Division, have been holding the perimeter. A courageous but progressively hopeless endeavour to buy time for the chaotic evacuation. When the order is finally given to cut and run, the regiment made an exhausting twenty mile forced march to the beach at Bray-Dunes. I am having trouble with the dates and cannot fix his experience in time. And yet, does it matter? If I do eventually trace an accurate chronological account of his regiment as they retreat to the beach will that help me to grasp the emotional impact of this experience on my father?

The only scrap of evidence I do have comes from an unknown source, certainly not my father, which suggests that for those days after the bomb, all he could eat was crushed up biscuits softened in water. It is a touching detail that rings true. It allows me to picture him painfully taking the standard army issue metal cup up to his lips which have the sunken look of extreme old age caused by the absence of his front teeth. It must be painful, causing him to protect the bloody cavities and stumps whilst sucking down the minimal nutritional value of some crushed army biscuits. Those army biscuits, I find, were:

"unsalted, hard, and dry, and were descended from the ships' biscuits and hard tack that military forces had used for centuries. They had little flavour, and were often called "tooth dullers".

The rudimentary military record I have found tells me that he was concussed. There is no mention of the teeth and yet to lose your teeth at such an early age must have been considerably more traumatic than a temporary concussion. I suppose it might be argued that the potential for long lasting brain damage was more serious than the purely cosmetic repercussions of losing all your teeth. But I can only think of my father, still just a teenager, and already known for his good looks, facing a life time of ill-fitting dentures which must be taken out at night and kept in a glass of water on the bedside table.

It is not hard to measure my own feelings against what I am certain he must have felt. Lucky to survive of course and fully aware that many of his fellow soldiers will have had quality of life destroying injuries, if they survived at all. He could have lost an arm or a leg or his face could have been truly disfigured. Worse, far worse, and yet I am fixated on the way he looked on those rare occasions when I would see him without his teeth. Those caved in lips adding years to his age and transforming his smile into a gaunt travesty of the face I knew. False teeth are not an affliction but I grieve for my father's teeth, smashed out on the dunes of *Bray-Dunes Plage* in amongst the fear and the desperation of a battle lost. I see him sitting up now sucking down his soggy biscuit gruel, feeling sorry for himself and yet maintaining, I am sure and against the laws of physics, a 'stiff upper lip'.

Drew Bethell aged 18 before embarking for France

CHAPTER 3

An Unexpected Graveyard

Hoo Peninsular Kent. April 10th 2022

This is Magwitch country in which the marshes are a: dark flat wilderness, intersected with dikes and mounds and gates, and the low leaden line beyond was the river; and that the distant savage lair from which the wind was rushing was the sea;

I am on the edge of the Thames estuary walking along a grassy track that Charles Dickens would have recognised. It runs along the edge of the marsh where Magwitch lurked. It is a grey day with dirty low-slung clouds obscuring the far shore of the River Medway revealing just a suggestion of the 19th century Hoo Fort, squat in the mist. The tide is out and it is easy to contemplate what dark and fearful remnants are buried in the grey suppurating mud holes that pockmark the clumps of scraggy grass and reeds. There is a promise of wraiths and shadows in this landscape, which is helpful as I am in search of ghosts. I am on my way to a graveyard.

As I round the bend in the track, I can make out what at

first looks like a series of dilapidated wooden sheds. They are clustered on the water's edge, random skeletal shapes. Old ribs and bones. Primordial. It is hard to discern a pattern or a rhythm to these fractured silhouettes. But as I approach the shapes resolve. The timeless curves of a hull with ribs agape are piled high. The stand posts and stumps of broken masts and stays. These are the decaying remains of once hard-working barges. This is where Thames barges come to die: abandoned, rotting and devoid of any dignity. I have arrived at the graveyard. Now I must try to discern the ghosts.

I abandoned my father at *Bray-Dune-Plage*, waiting with tens of thousands of others to be picked up off the beach and taken home. I know that he got home: he must have done. A few of the stragglers were rounded up by the Wehrmacht and marched off to spend the next four years in dismal work camps in central Europe. But as we will see, my father went on to serve in Africa and was captured and escaped and returned to fight his way up Italy. For him the war was by no means over. But how he got off that beach still suffering from concussion and with a bleeding toothless mouth, I had no clue.

Then, an online search gave me an unexpected glimpse of what might have happened. A thread to follow. My father's regiment, the 19th Field is almost invisible in the hundreds of pages of testimony and historical reporting of the extraction of the BEF from the beaches of Northern France. And yet when I searched on the name of the regiment and 'Dunkirk' there was a result. An unlikely source: the website of the *Little Ships of Dunkirk*; a celebration of all the smaller craft that became synonymous with what would be perceived as a national triumph rather than a military disaster.

The blog post referred to the Thames barge Ena which, on the 31st May 1940, headed across the channel with three other barges.

> *The Ena survived the one-hundred-mile outward journey across the English Channel which was strewn with mines. During their crossing they endured constant air attacks. Finally, Alfred Page, her skipper was ordered to beach her close to the smaller sand barge H.A.C. As the Germans closed in, the crews of both barges were ordered to abandon their ships and escape on a minesweeper to England.*

That should have been the end of the story. A futile journey with no clear reason given as to why the skipper was ordered to abandon the Ena. However, there was more to come:

> *There are two eye-witness accounts of what happened next. Alex Smith recalls how he, with thirty men of the Duke of Wellington's regiment commanded by Captain David Strangeways their Adjutant, arrived on La Panne beach. They could not believe their luck when they saw two barges in seaworthy condition anchored and almost afloat.*

Now, the Duke of Wellington's regiment was part of the 1st Division along with my father's regiment. *La Panne* beach is just up the coast from *Bray-Dunes-Plage* I am getting warmer. These could be real actors in my father's story. The eye witness account goes on:

> *They took possession of the barge H.A.C. while Colonel McKay with his men of the 19th Field Regiment, Royal Artillery boarded the Ena which was beached not far away.*

Colonel McKay was my father's commanding officer. I have since discovered he was a friend of the family and the reason Drew ended up in 19th Field. It is very plausible that he would have kept an eye on Drew. If they were both evacuated aboard the *Ena* then I have the next and final part of my father's Dunkirk story. I am elated. This is historical evidence not mere creative conjecture. I have made progress, piecing together my father's story. And yet, I am worried. My father was wounded, could he have made it out to the anchored barge wading, then swimming, and then heaving himself over the side? It seems unlikely and yet that second eye-witness account gives me fresh hope.

> *Meanwhile, Captain Atley of the East Yorkshire Regiment, was on the beach and together with one of his men, quickly made a raft. Using shovels, they rowed out to the Ena, and helped thirty-six other men on board including three wounded.*

Including three wounded! There were wounded men on the

barge. Let us go with the flow. My father escaped from the beach in the Thames barge *Ena*. Not that it was an easy journey back.

> *By 8am both barges were under way. Then, according to Alex Smith, the two ships got involved in one of the most remarkable barge races of all time. Under constant enemy bombardment and machine-gun fire, they crossed the Channel. Captain Atley recalls that by midnight they took a back-bearing on Dunkirk and found they had gone too far south-west. His only sailing experience had been on the Broads and he had forgotten to put the leeboards down. So, they altered course to north-northwest and finally sighted the North Goodwin buoy. They then had to tack again towards the South Goodwin lightship. Eventually, the Ena was picked up by a tug or fleet auxiliary and taken into Margate.*

It is not surprising they stray twenty miles in the wrong direction. The captain and crew, experienced Thames barge sailors, had abandoned their command and so the one hundred or so men on board were in the hands of a couple of amateur sailors whose only experience was sailing on the Norfolk Broads. And yet, another minor miracle gets my father home.

They eventually end up in Margate and now I am trying to imagine my father on the pier beneath where the Turner Gallery stands today. I have visited and looked out on the harbour but with no connection to the place. Now it will resonate with my family history. A place of significance. It seems Margate was second only to Dover as a destination for the evacuating ships and boats. A long working pier and a railway station close by made it ideal for processing the troops.

> *By the 29th May, the evacuation began to move into overdrive and at its height there were fifty-plus vessels waiting off Margate to dock at the pier or harbour and discharge their human cargo.*

Men of 19th Field Regiment were part of that cargo.

I see my father lying on the deck: he like all the men on that barge is spent. Look at the newsreel footage and you see men whose compelling instinct for self-preservation has been dulled into submission. And yet they smile. They smile at the camera and those that did not smile will be left on the cutting room floor. For the wheels are in motion to turn what was clearly a spectacular disaster into a national triumph. Wherever they could cameramen would capture a smile, a cheeky wave and chirpy chappie to embody the new interpretation that will last for decades (and even fuel another disastrous withdrawal, Brexit). In reality I feel sure that all the desperate energy required to get them off that beach has long since dissipated. The intermittent bursts of adrenalin caused by the sound of enemy planes harassing the *Ena* as it made its way across the channel have taken their toll. And yet there is relief.

They have survived. My father has survived. I try to picture him, , sitting patiently on the deck of the Ena as she rolls in the swell outside the harbour walls waiting for a space to open up on the dock. I am searching for his face amongst the men crammed in beside him Is that him lying with his head propped up against a hawser coiled around a stanchion post? His mouth will still be painful, his gums and the broken stumps will have nerves open to the cold. They say that we disproportionally feel pain in the face. It is hard to ignore and it mingles with the distorted self-image it forces upon us. If you have lost all your teeth, not only are you in pain, you are also humiliated. Your sense of how you look to others is grossly distorted. I can feel his distress, his vulnerability and his yearning for some tender care and restoration. He is after all just nineteen years of age: still a boy, already damaged by a man's war.

> *Among the returning soldiers were many wounded. Serious casualties were despatched to the Royal Sea Bathing Hospital or Margate General Hospital for treatment. Those suffering from more superficial wounds were attended to by one of the First Aid stations established at Dreamland.*

When I was a young teacher in Hackney we used to take our charges on a summer outing to Margate. I recall many frustrating hours chasing recalcitrant teenagers around Dreamland in and out of the decrepit fairground attractions. That memory is now transformed by the image of my father lying on a makeshift hospital bed whilst, for the first time, a doctor treats his mouth and checks his vitals. All is well. Like me he will have been able to hear the trains from inside Dreamland, the station is right next door. If he was passed fit to travel he would have been guided up the slope to the station.

> *In the booking hall of the station, a free canteen was set up by the Mayor and around fifty women of the town. Soldiers were provided with tea and food and, each soldier was given a packet of biscuits, a bar of chocolate and an apple for the journey.*

That bar of chocolate must have tasted good even if he did have to suck it down.

I am looking up at the transom of the very barge that I want to believe brought my father back from Dunkirk. The paint is peeling. On one side the word ENA and on the other, the word IPSWICH. The words are painted onto a blue scroll which twirls under itself. An artistic touch. They would certainly have been painted over numerous times and yet, as I stand with my boots sinking into the seaweed and sludge, I wonder whether my father read those same words on a similar blue scroll as they rowed him out on the raft and helped him over the side and onto the oak decking, which I can just see from my vantage point.

Now, in 2024, the craft is rotting away despite the sturdiness of its construction. It has been abandoned with several other Thames barges on the side of the River Medway. They have been left to rot in the black mud that sucks at every step I take. It is low tide so the hulks do not have the bilge grey water of the Medway to hide the humiliating gashes in their once stalwart bodies. They are fully exposed in all their putrefying misery. The Ena still has some vestiges of her robust construction. From where I stand, the hull seems largely intact, curving away to reveal the flat bottom that allowed Captain Page to bring her in so close to the beach that she eventually ran aground. However, as I move around to the other side, a yawning gash in the hull is partially covered by a shard of tattered blue tarpaulin. It allows me to see inside, into the lower decks that might have been a safer haven for my wounded father.

I want so much to feel the significance of this festering hulk. I want to experience some emotional engagement with its history. I half close my eyes and try to raise the ghost of my father and the rest of the 19th Field Regiment, Royal Artillery heading back to Margate on the morning of June 2nd 1940. The records speak of some one hundred men so they would have been jammed tight, huddled together on the deck with faces turned up to the sky in anxious anticipation. Or maybe a combination of relief at getting off that damned beach and extreme exhaustion would have them resigned to whatever else the crazy war can throw at them. Could they be sleeping? I can see them now. Battle dress blouses buttoned to the neck with revolving shank buttons. Trousers tucked into webbing anklets, with pockets on the thigh: one for a map and one for a first aid kit. I am familiar with those khaki serge uniforms, I know the feel from my days as a cadet at my public school in the sixties when we were dressed in cast-offs from that same conflict. I know that when those tunics got wet and muddy just how they smelt and how they chaffed on bare skin.

I am pleased to have tracked down Ena. I feel I have made an unlikely connection with my father. I feel confident that had I bothered to engage in a similar search before he died (in 1988, long before we were gifted with the power of Google Search) that he would have accompanied me down the A 20 and that we would have talked about his recollections of that time. Man to man. As we parked the car just outside the village of Hoo ('Dad, that church yard, it's the one where Magwitch accosted Pip in the first chapter of Great Expectations') he too would have felt the same frisson of anticipation that I had experienced as I clambered up the sea wall and caught my first glimpse of the decaying hulks. I want to think that he would. I want to imagine that I would have asked him whether he recognised the Ena, and how it made him feel. And I want him to be just a little overwhelmed as the memories came flooding back. I would like him to emote, to explain and to satisfy my desire to know just what he went through.

The Ena grounded on the beach at La Panne.

Ena in the Thames Barge graveyard, Hoo, Kent

Stoke Newington, London February 2024

Dear Dad,

It is hard to know what you would make of my creative re-enactment of your time on the beach at Dunkirk. I can only surmise. I think you would have been flattered that I had at least tried to imagine what it was like for you. I like to think that if only I had not left it so late, you and I could have taken a trip out to the Thames barge graveyard and found the Ena. Even though you would have enjoyed the excitement of discovery, I fear you would have doubted your own memories. You would protest: it was so long ago, you were so young and actually you could easily have been evacuated by some other means. By your own account, when you were alive, your memory was untrustworthy. In that sense it was probably better that you weren't there when I came upon the barges. I had no one to challenge my myth making. I could take the credit for some pretty decent detective work. Others would be impressed. My generation have grown to savour the discovery of our links to the wartime past of our relatives.

If I am right and you would have been resistant to endorsing my creative re-enactment, I have to wonder whether you really had buried those memories. I know you subscribed to the view, along with much of your generation, that 'digging around in the past' was counterproductive. You were the victim of extreme trauma and you were very young, and yet for you it was better to 'let those sleeping dogs lie'. I, of course, would counter that the dogs were not sleeping and the events of a traumatic past will impact behaviour in the present. Although I do remember you telling me that your generation never knew what trauma meant and that during the war it was survival that counted. And, of course, you had survived. That was what mattered. And God knows I have no right to challenge that.

I think about myself at the age of nineteen. I thought I was pretty daring hitch hiking around North America during the summer of race riots. I had a few scary moments, but there was never a threat to my life or my well-being. I find it impossible to imagine myself on that beach. Likely to die at any moment or somehow worse, to be horribly wounded.

When we did talk about your generation, which wasn't often, you claimed that what made it easier was the expectations that you would obey your elders and betters. I think you would argue that it was discipline that meant that so many of you got off that beach. You did what you were told. You didn't jump the queue. I think you would have intimated that my generation might not have waited in line. For days. Watching as men were killed all around us.

I honestly don't know. I like to think that we would not have disgraced ourselves. But then, you were right, there were different expectations. We had it easier. I suppose you could say we were softer. Certainly, more comfortable. We weren't anticipating hardship or risk on that scale. We were lucky. Your generation had fought the battles and you were parented by a survivor of the First World War.. So, after the war we were benefitting. You would say that we were encouraged to be selfish.

And that's my problem Dad. You had been hardened up by your upbringing, your school and your training. You once told me that 'One wasn't taught to talk about oneself'. On the other hand, you were happy to talk about some things. Just not the difficult or traumatic things in your life. It's why I think you were able to talk about your escape and the walk down Italy, because it was an adventure. There was no trauma. But when it comes to Dunkirk: not a word. Was it just too difficult to remember? Did you bury that memory because it was too painful?

But now I am going to take us back to the beginning. We are going back to your early childhood. I have decided to ghost write your autobiography. I am going to fabricate a first-person account: perhaps it is a dishonest tactic. However, if I resort to the third person to the formal biographical voice, I will be intimating that somehow there is a factual truth: a deeply researched set of evidence. But there is no such thing. Yet again I am taking liberties with your history.

Yours was a colonial upbringing. Africa in the twenties was a rough place to be maintaining the empire, already showing signs of fraying at the edges. We did not have the automatic hegemony of the British Raj. Every major European state was exploiting the resources and imposing its language and cultural norms. Britain could not always rely on its 'manifest destiny' to make life easy for its colonial servants.

2024

This ghost-written autobiography will take you up to the summer of 1935. You are fourteen years old: the innocent abroad. You are visiting your parents in Gibraltar. I will be joining you there on the day your world turned upside down.

Love

Hum.

CHAPTER 4
A Ghost-Written Autobiography

From Dar es Salam to Gibraltar, 1921 to 1935

I was born on Sunday 6th February 1921 at the Ocean Road Hospital[1], Dar es Salam, in Tanganyika Territory (then known as German East Africa). It was my father's first posting after joining the Colonial Service at the end of the First World War. He had been wounded in the last months of the war but had made a full recovery.[2] Before the war he had been a bank clerk so it was not surprising that he was charged with managing finance in the colonies. East Africa was not an easy station especially for my mother who had been brought up in Canada. In Winnipeg, where the winters were savagely cold.

I remember very little about Dar es Salam. I am certain that we were looked after by a nanny, who would have been a local woman. I don't think we would have seen very much of my

---

[1.] The hospital still exists and the buildings include many that date back to the British Colonial period. It is up the road from the government buildings where Drew's father would have worked as an Assistant Treasurer. It is unlikely that he would have attended the birth of his first born.

[2.] Donald Bethell was wounded on September 25 1918 at the battle of Bourlon Wood one of the last big battles of the war. He was shot in the thigh and the little finger. He was discharged from hospital with the note that he had: *no appreciable disabilities from wounds.*

father who was socially very active: he was an active swimmer and a keen golfer and enjoyed the colonial social life to the full.

Some eighteen months after I was born, my brother Tony arrived. We were very close in age and I have no memory of him as a baby. We grew up together and must have been good company for each other, as I don't believe there were many English families out there. It was a remote posting.

In 1925 my father was promoted to Senior Assistant Treasurer and posted to Berbera in British Somaliland[3]. I was four years old and Tony was barely three. I can remember the house we lived in but little else. There was a garden and we were quite close to a lovely beach, I seem to remember our nanny regularly took us down there to swim and build sand castles[4]. In September 1929, at the age of eight, I was sent back to England to go to boarding school. I had to come back by ship. I can remember coming through the Suez Canal. I think my mother came with me although I cannot be sure. I started at Junior Kings School, in Sturry, outside Canterbury. It was a substantial Tudor house with eighty acres of land that ran down to the River Stour[5]. My mother left me there at the start of term. I must have been homesick for a while but you soon get used to being away from your parents. I can remember plenty of outdoor activities although I am not sure I was very good at sport, at least not as

---

[3] Winston Churchill described Berbera as: "unproductive, inhospitable, and the people were very hostile to the occupation". He also stated that the governor's residence "was unfit for a decent English dog".

[4] "Berbera is also bound by sweeping beaches, about 3km from the centre, including Baathela Beach, just in front of Maan-soor Hotel. At dawn, dolphins can be seen frolicking in the bay". *Lonely Planet Guide.*

[5] The building was opened by Rudyard Kipling who wrote of the importance of filling "the unforgiving minutes with sixty seconds of distance run" (sic)

good as my brother. He joined the school in 1930 and I remember he was very athletic from the start.

We only got to visit our family once a year for the summer holidays. We spent the other holidays with my mother's cousin who lived in the New Forest. I remember the ships that took us out to Africa. That was an adventure in itself. I also remember how pleased we were to see my mother. My father was very busy so we did not see much of him.

In the same year that Tony came to school with me, my father was again promoted. This time he took on the prestigious role of Colonial Treasurer and Collector in the British Overseas Territory of Gibraltar. He was just thirty-two years old. He clearly had a stellar career ahead of him. Within a couple of years, he had taken on further duties: he was a member of the Executive Council, Justice of the Peace, Commissioner of State Duties, and Commissioner of Currency.

We lived in a grand house high up on the Rock. It came with the job and had a fine garden. It was a prestigious address and many of the senior figures in the colonial and military administration lived up there. There was a very active social life. My parents were often out at parties. My father was very active in the Swimming Club and the Golf Club, but his real passion was for the races. He was on the committee of the Civilian Racing Club. I don't remember being taken to the races, in fact I don't think my mother went. It was my father's world. I certainly think he enjoyed a bet.

In 1934, I moved from prep school to Sherborne School in Dorset. I was allocated to Harper House one of the seven boarding houses. It was a spartan place in those days. I remember having cold showers every morning even in the dead of winter. I adapted well to life there. My housemaster was a man called Barlow who was pretty decent. Most of the discipline was left up to the prefects and I suppose I must have been beaten fairly often. Not that I was a trouble maker. The school was very focussed on sports and as I matured physically I found I was not too bad and could hold my own on the rugby field. I especially enjoyed gymnastics and I was an even better swimmer.

As before, we spent the winter holidays with family in England. Then at the end of the summer term we would go down to Southampton and board a P&O liner for the week-long voyage down to Gibraltar. Usually the ships were bound for India and were very well appointed. My brother and I had fun as there was always something to do: deck games, concerts and plenty of good food. We had the run of the ship although sometimes we would get into trouble for straying into the First-Class deck as we were in the Second-Class cabins.

I remember the voyage we took in the summer of 1935. Tony had been appointed Head Boy at our prep school and he was pretty cocky. I seem to remember he had his eye on a girl in First Class. He was still thirteen and I was fourteen, but he seemed to have already developed a way with the ladies. We were looking forward to our holidays. We had just over two months to enjoy ourselves. And of course, we hadn't seen our mother or father for nine months. We were especially looking forward to seeing our young brother Denis who had been just four months old when we saw him the summer before.

CHAPTER 5

A Death on the Rock

THE GIBRALTAR CHRONICLE
JULY 22ND, 1935

OBITUARY
The Hon. D. L. Bethell

We deeply regret to report the death of the Hon. D.L. Bethell J.P. which occurred at the Treasury yesterday morning in tragic circumstances.

He enjoyed a wide popularity, and every member of the community will join in extending to Mrs Bethell and her three sons, the youngest of whom was born in Gibraltar, profound sympathy in the great sorrow that has fallen on them.

Mr Bethell was only 40 years of age. He came to Gibraltar as Colonial Treasurer and Collector in October 1931 and was a Member of the Executive

Council, Justice of the Peace, Commissioner of Currency and President of the Tender Board.

Apart from his public services Mr. Bethell took a leading part in the social life of Gibraltar. Always active and keen on games, he represented the Colonial Civil Service on the Committee of the United Sports Club, being also on the Committee of the Officers Swimming Club and the Golf Club. An enthusiastic race-goer, he was almost invariably present at the meetings of the Jockey Club and Civilian Racing Club, being Vice President of the latter.

At the conclusion of the inquest yesterday, the Hon. Attorney General said: "I wish to express deepest and heartfelt sympathy with the widow and all the members of the family of the late Mr Bethell. He was a man who was held in high esteem by all who came in contact with him in every walk of life. By his sad and untimely death, the Colonial Service and Gibraltar lost a trusted and much valued officer".

CHAPTER 6

A Normal School Holiday Morning

50 Europa Road, Gibraltar, Friday July 21st, 1935

Even during the summer holidays, Beaulieu House was a place of routines. I am the time traveller watching my grandfather Donald appear at the dining table at 7.40 am sharp, as he has always done. He allows himself twenty minutes to take breakfast and prepare himself for the day ahead. He is on his own, as he always is. His wife is still upstairs. That is the way he likes it. He relishes the space to take stock and rehearse the upcoming events of his day. He is dressed for the office in a summer suit of soft brown linen, with a cream silk shirt and a Racing Club of Gibraltar tie.

Amina, the Spanish maid, brings in a plate of bacon and eggs, a bowl of fruit, toast and a small pot of coffee, but unusually, Donald pushes the plate away. Equally unusually, he has not smiled at Amina, who lowers her eyes as she reclaims the plate. She offers up the toast, but that too is refused. Donald pours himself a cup of coffee and picks at the bowl of pineapple and sliced orange. If I were able to interview Amina, she would have commented on his desultory mood and how uncommon it was in her master who was invariably full of energy and good humour.

I, of course, will be looking for clues and notice that he begins to scan the front page of the Gibraltar Chronicle but loses interest and instead stares out of the bay window to his right that looks out over the garden where the serried ranks of planted classical urns are throwing dark morning shadows across the gravel. Amina asks if he needs anything else and he musters a half smile as he shakes his head.

At 7.58 a black Wolseley Wasp draws up outside the portico that, although modest, denotes the status of a house that was in keeping with the post of Colonial Treasurer. The driver gets out and gives the bonnet and headlamps an extra polish as a way to pass the time. Meanwhile Donald has risen from the table as he always does on the arrival of his car and again, according to well-worn routine, enters the hallway to collect his briefcase and hat, and calls up to his wife who by now is standing at the top of the stairs. The bright morning sunshine from the window behind her causes her to glow in her white cotton voile dress. Her face is in shadow. Donald admires his wife and usually offers her a flattering and teasing remark. Today he merely smiles as she reminds him that he needs to be back by half past five as they are due at the Governor's Residence at six for cocktails before going on to the Civilian Racing Club ball where Donald is Vice President and will need to give a short speech of welcome.

"Of course, my love. I'll be back in good time. Can you make sure that Amina puts out my dinner jacket and the miniature medals?"

"I am having coffee with Lady Robertson this morning. Will you get back for lunch? The boys would love to see you".

"I don't think so. Maybe tomorrow. It's very busy at the moment and I am hoping to fit in a game of tennis with Jonnie Rosso this afternoon".

He turns, picks up his briefcase and then his soft fedora hat which he puts on with care. He checks in the mirror, adjusts the angle and moves out into the harsh light of the morning.

I am looking at his expression. I am looking for signs of distress. Because I am the time traveller I know that he has made plans for his own demise, but I am damned if I see any outwards signs of an inner turmoil.

Next to arrive at the breakfast table is Tony, just thirteen years old and even though I only remember him in his fifties and beyond, I can recognize his square face and narrow eyes. In contrast to his father on this particular morning, he is full of energy. The fourteen-year-old Jessica Carlton-Smythe has invited him for a sail round the bay on the family yacht. He has been angling for just such an invitation and is excited at the prospect. And just as he starts on his third piece of toast heavily loaded with Seville marmalade, a motor horn sounds from the bottom of the drive and he abandons the toast. He dashes into the hall where his mother is talking to Catalina, the nanny, who is holding his eighteen-month-old brother Denis.

"Where are you off to in such a hurry?"

"I told you. I am sailing with the Carlton Smythe's. And they are waiting at the gate. I've got to rush."

"Will you be back for lunch?"

"It's just a trip around the bay. I'll be back by one. As long as they give me a lift."

"Take care, darling."

But Tony is already out of the door and running down the drive.

As my grandmother turns her attention back to Catalina, Drew, my father, starts to descend the ornate stairs. He is more measured in his descent. He is pleased to see his baby brother and takes him from the nanny. He is confident holding him high and engaging in un-self-conscious baby talk. Denis chuckles.

Drew wears long soft flannel trousers and a white shirt with his sleeves rolled up to the elbows. He is tall for his age but not out of proportion. I do not recognize any of my physical disproportion. At his age I was a gangly and uncoordinated youth but he seems comfortable in his skin. When he gets to the dining room, he offers Amina a generous smile and a *'Buenos dias, Amina. Como estas?"*. I recognise the man who, throughout his life, was always learning enough of a foreign language to put others at their ease. Amina clearly appreciates his uncomplicated charm and smiles back warmly.

His morning is less social. He plans to walk down the hill to the military garrison where he has made friends with the son of the commanding officer. They will spend the morning watching the men training to use the new heavy artillery that has recently been installed to defend the Straits. Drew is already interested in the mechanics of war. He feels comfortable amongst soldiers and his time in the Sherborne School CCF has already inspired him to consider a career in the army.

It is lunchtime. In the dining room Drew is sitting opposite his mother, my grandmother, in the seat that, had he returned for lunch, his father would have occupied. As the elder son he is eligible for the privilege. There is a place set for Tony, but at this moment he has not made good on his promise to be 'back by one'. Amina has brought in the chicken salad and Drew is regaling his mother with an account of the range and explosive load of the new guns.

I, on the other hand, am standing outside in the shade of the portico anxiously looking out for an unwelcome visitation. I am expecting the imminent arrival of the Wolseley Wasp, and I know that this time it will not be the Colonial Treasurer sitting in the back seat. It will be Mr Baricasas, the Assistant Treasurer. The bearer of bad news. After a brief wait I can now hear the sound of a car turning into the drive and making its way up the gravel drive towards the house.

Back in the dining room, Drew also hears the unanticipated arrival of the Wolseley. He turns to look out of the window. He assumes his father is back for a late lunch. He will need to move his seat. Kay looks up from her chicken salad. She was sure that she heard Donald say he would not be coming back for lunch. She wonders aloud whether it might be the van from MacKinnon's delivering the groceries she had ordered earlier in the day. But as it passes the window she too is confused and presses the bell for Amina. They will need another plate of chicken salad and a glass of sherry, her husband's lunchtime indulgence when he does make it home.

The Wolsely draws up at the front door. I step back to disguise my presence (not that there is any need, I am there in spirit only). The driver is quick to get out and move round to open the door for his passenger. But Mr Baricasas is in no rush, indeed he seems loath to disembark. I can see his face now and I see the haunted look of a man who wishes above all things not be in this place, at this time bearing a message that will surely set off an emotional cataclysm in this family that he knows only from the most formal of occasions, but for whom he has developed a high regard.

It is now clear to Mrs Bethell that this is neither the grocery delivery nor the unexpected return of her husband. She is not yet anxious. She has known the car to be sent to collect a forgotten piece of sporting equipment (Did he take his tennis racket? She could not remember) or a set of formal clothes for an unexpected meeting with the Governor. She sends Amina off to see who it is and inquire as to what they want. She waits patiently. Drew is up and looking out of the bay window.

"It's the Assistant Treasurer. What's his name? What's he doing here.?"

That piece of intelligence causes a thin shimmer of anxiety in my grandmother. This is very unusual. She can think of no logical reason why the Assistant Treasurer would come up to Beaulieu House. It is so unlikely. Something was wrong with the certainties that governed their lives. Something is out of kilter and her mind has started to race. As Amina re-enters the dining room, she too can sense that there is something out of order. Her life too is governed by order.

"Mr Baricasas would like to speak with you, Ma'am. Alone"

This last word hangs in the air. Drew hears it and Kay hears it too. It resonates. For Drew it feels like a rejection: an assertion that at fourteen he is not able to join the grown-ups. For his mother it is altogether more sinister. It taps straight into a well-hidden anxiety that perhaps her husband's assurance that his 'modest' bets on the races ("I have to show willing dear, I am Vice President after all") are in fact far from modest and the losses have been revealed.

Watching them from the hallway, I also understand the full import of that last word. I know why she must face this moment alone. I know the explosive news that Mr Baricasas is about to impart.

"Thank you, Amina. Please show him into the drawing room."

There is a pause. A hiatus whilst Kay gathers herself and allows time for Mr Baricasas to be introduced into the drawing room. She is breathing deeply and I can see her as she walks across the hall. Her step is hesitant as if she is considering an alternative destination. An avoidance. But she continues to the drawing room door.

"Good afternoon, Mr Baricasas. What a pleasant surprise. Do sit down".

We can hear her voice fade and crack slightly as it reaches the end of that sentence. She shuts the door firmly.

By now Drew is in the hall. He, like me, heard her voice fade as she finishes the invitation to sit down. It is clear to me that she has seen the look on his face. My father does not know what to think. He has witnessed so few family crises. He has been away from the home for most of the last seven years. He is not yet filled with dread. He is curious and just a little apprehensive. Amina's presence requires him to resist the temptation to move across the hall and place his ear against the door. All he can hear are the indistinct tones of a disembodied voice.

I now see the anxious look of a boy who fears there are forces at work over which he will have little agency. I know there is a maelstrom about to break and I am helpless to protect my father. My interest is heightened because I know that in forty-five years' time he will receive news of the untimely death of his own son and the shock and the trauma will be just as intense.

As I am focussing all my attention on my father, my uncle

Tony charges up the stairs. He is flushed with the excitement of his sailing trip around the bay and is bright in anticipation of sharing the details with his brother and his mother. But his enthusiastic bubble is deflated the moment he reaches the hall and catches sight of his brother and Amina. They have drained the oxygen out of the air and Tony slides to a stop. He has noticed the presence of the Wolsely outside the front door but it did not impinge on his dash for lunch and a chance to share his adventure. Now, he spins back to look at the car and then turns back to his brother who motions towards the closed drawing room door. Although his head is full of questions, he has intuited that the situation calls for a respectful silence. He is confident that all will be revealed in good time.

A moment later and the brothers hear their mother let out a sound that neither have ever heard before. Half sob, half cry of alarm. Up until this moment their mother has hidden all outward displays of extreme emotion, so this alien dissonance cuts through the warm reassuring atmosphere of the hallway with its smell of pot-pourri and beeswax polish. It injects a sharp stab of primal fear. The boys remain fixed to the spot. Amina makes a strangled cry of her own as her eyes widen and then her hand covers her mouth. She backs away and disappears into the back of the house, to the kitchen: she knows she needs to be elsewhere.

Now they can hear sobbing and they cannot stop themselves from approaching the door. But before they get too close, the door opens suddenly and Mr Bacarisa stands square in the doorway. The boys try to look round him to see their mother, but he has other plans and moves firmly forward and manages to close the door behind him. Drew, being the tallest does in fact catch sight of his mother sat on the sofa with her head in her hands. But it is just a glimpse. Now he must turn his attention to the Assistant Treasurer, who is holding his bowler hat in front of him with two hands, as protection.

"Your mother has just received some very bad news and she would like you to phone Mrs Wilson Smith and ask her to come around just as soon as she can."

Drew hesitates, but the imperative of his mother's command overcomes his desperate desire to know more. He moves to the Bakelite phone on the camphor wood dresser brought back from Dar es Salaam. He dials, each number requiring that tense wait for the finger wheel to make its way back from the stop, it cannot be rushed and the Wilson Smith number is made up of many high digits.

There is a pause whilst the connection is made.

"Good afternoon. Could I please speak to Mrs Wilson-Smith? It is Drew Bethell. It's rather urgent"

Another pause, whilst the maid finds the mistress of the house.

"Hello, is that Mrs Wilson Smith? Yes, it's Drew Bethell. Yes, I'm fine thank you. Um, I am ringing because my mother has had some bad news and she has asked whether you could come round. . . I am not exactly sure. But. . . she seems upset. . . very upset. . . Thank you. Yes of course.".

He puts the phone down and turns back to Mr Baricasas.

"She says she will come over."

"I shall wait"

"Can we go in and see my mother?"

"I think it might be better to leave her until Mrs Wilson Smith arrives. I believe she also lives on Europa Road, so she should not be too long." Dealing with a woman *in extremis* is clearly considered women's work.

What follows is an agonising stasis. For ten minutes Mr Baricasas stands holding his bowler hat, shifting from one shiny black brogue to the other. The boys too are stuck, standing in limbo. There is nothing to say. There is nothing to do. Once in a while they can hear the subdued sounds of what must be their mother in distress, but they are so far removed from the habitual expectations of their roles and responses that they are frozen in the excruciating moment.

After ten interminable minutes, Mrs Wilson Smith arrives. She has walked up. She is breathing deeply and a light perspiration shines on her forehead. She surveys the scene. She hardly recognises the boys who she knows well. She is expecting the warm courtesy, for which Drew at least, is famous.

There is no smile rather the starkly strained look of a boy who knows that his life is likely to be turned upside down but cannot understand how.

Mrs Wilson plays safe and walks up to Mr Baricasas expecting an explanation and some orientation: something to help her engage with the situation. But he too is silenced: he cannot start to explain whilst the boys are there. He cannot be the one to tell them their father is dead. Not there. That is way beyond what he sees as his duty. He has fulfilled those obligations by informing the wife. He is prepared to breach the polite expectations of the moment and remain silent in the company of a woman he is hoping will release him from his obligation. He merely indicates the door to the drawing room with an apologetic shrug.

Mrs Wilson Smith enters the drawing room and closes the door, leaving the three males in further suspended animation. Mr Baricasas is the first to break ranks. He approaches the two brothers who are expecting some indication of what has happened, but the Assistant Treasurer merely puts out his hand. Drew realises what is required, he shakes the proffered hand and then feels the need to say something.

"Thank you"

"I am so sorry. We will do all that we can to help. Now I must return to the office. There is much to do".

After a more cursory handshake with Tony, Mr Baricasas

heads for the door. He knows he should not show any sign of relief or urgency and yet he wants to leave this house. He has brought news that will devastate the emotional equilibrium and he can do nothing that will alleviate the impact. He has no language or protocol that will help him to leave with an appropriate gravitas. So, he puts on his bowler hat and moves swiftly down the steps and into the back seat of the car. The boys follow him out. They feel it is their duty to see him off the premises. It was what their father would have done.

I am still watching, and of course I am concentrating on my father. For Drew, as the first born, will be expected to step up as head of the family in a household where his mother has been abandoned and where her status in a highly status-conscious society will diminish by the day. She is about to be denied his salary, her only source of income. She is living in grand accommodation tied to her husband's job and will be required to leave. She is looking at the prospect of making her way in the world on a meagre widow's pension. She has three boys to look after, two of whom attend an expensive public school where the fees have been largely subsidised by the Colonial Service. Her third child an afterthought, maybe even a mistake, is just eighteen months old and has been looked after, almost entirely by a nanny made possible with another subsidy from her husband's employers. Of course, my father, aged fourteen, has no idea what lies ahead. He still does not know what has happened. He cannot compute the bizarre sequence of events. And yet he knows that something has changed and, even, that things will never be the same again.

The brothers return to the hallway as Mrs Wilson Smith reappears from the drawing room. She is diminished. She has lost the initial patina of assurance that she brought to the household. And yet she must explain to the boys that their father is dead. A sudden, unexpected death. Will she explain the circumstances of his death? I am not sure. I am trying to reconstruct the conversation where you tell two teenagers that their father shot himself in the head and I have fallen short. It is quite enough to process the cold hard fact that you no longer have a father. Do you need to know the details of his demise? I am not even certain that my father ever knew exactly what happened on that sunny morning in the Treasury. Would he have read the Inquest Report that appeared in the Gibraltar Chronicle on Tuesday July 22nd 1935?

Mr. Donald L.. Bethell

Mrs. Donald Bethell

1935

Drew and Tony Bethell at the time of their father's death.

CHAPTER 7
The Coroner's Inquest

THE GIBRALTAR CHRONICLE,
MONDAY JULY 23ND, 1935

At the Colonial Hospital yesterday afternoon before Mr Albert R. Isola JP, acting as Coroner, an enquiry was held into the circumstances attending the death of Hon. D.L. Bethell.

The first witness was Dr J. E. Deale, Acting Colonial Surgeon, who was summoned to the Treasury about midday, where he found the deceased lying on the floor with a bullet wound in the side of his head, life being extinct. The wound had been caused by a shot from a firearm at close quarters. The bullet which has inflicted the injury was fired by an automatic pistol which was found near the body and in which there were three other cartridges of similar type. The wound could have been self-inflicted or caused by another person holding a revolver close to the head.

Mr F.P. Galliano, clerk in the Treasury, was then called and said that about 11.20 on Friday he was in the Correspondence Office on the first floor when he heard a bang, followed by another like a door banging but did not suspect that anything was wrong. With the windows and doors open, all kinds of street noises could be heard in the Treasury. Shortly afterwards a caller asked for the Treasurer, who was found to be out of his office although his hat was on his desk, and after waiting some time the caller had to leave to keep an appointment. Subsequently witness went into the office several times, and about 11.55 am went through the office and tried the door of the lavatory in an adjoining passage which he found to be closed. Witness described how, after consulting Mr Bacarisa the Assistant Treasurer, he eventually discovered the body behind the door. In reply to the Coroner, witness said that he had spoken to Mr Bethell several times during the morning when he appeared to be just the same as on other days.

Mr H.E. Baricasas, Assistant Treasurer, gave similar evidence regarding the noises and the steps taken before and after the discovery of the body. At the end of the passage previously referred to there was a private door leading to Line Wall, which was used by the Treasurer himself but this was always locked. He had never seen the revolver before. Mr Bethell had a private safe in his office but the keys were kept on the same bunch as those of the strong room. Questioned by the Coroner, witness said that he had noticed nothing abnormal about the deceased, with whom he was in close contact daily.

The Hon. H. R Hone, Attorney General, who represented the Government at the enquiry, asked this witness, in view of his constant and close association with the deceased, whether everything was in order. Mr Baricasas replied that an official survey since the occurrence had shown everything to be in order.

Mr Frederick Hurd, messenger in the Treasury, said that deceased looked rather drawn that morning, and he not greeted witness with his usual smile.

Mr H.E.C. Merrick, Colonial Auditor, gave evidence that after obtaining, from the bank the Government pass-book, which had been brought up to date, he and Mr Baricasas had checked the Treasury cash accounts and found them correct. The investigation had found all public accounts to be in order.

Mr W.S. Gulloch, Chief of Police, described the Police investigation and said that both windows of the lavatory were intact and barred in such a way as to prevent entrance. A packet containing cartridges similar to those in the pistol had been found in the deceased's private safe which was unlocked, but there were not papers or letters which could throw any light on the occurrence.

The Coroner said that he did not propose to call any further witnesses and after a short adjournment, announces that he would record a version of suicide whilst of unsound mind. He expressed his deepest sympathy with the widow and family of the deceased.

CHAPTER 8

The Funeral

GIBRALTAR CHRONICLE.
AUGUST 4TH, 1935

THE FUNERAL OF THE HON. D. L. BETHELL

'The funeral of the Hon D.L. Bethell took place on Saturday morning from his residence in Europa Road. The coffin was covered with the Union Jack and was borne on a gun carriage. There were many magnificent wreaths including one from the Governor General Sir Charles Harington-Harington. In the procession were detachments of the Civil Police and Revenue Officers and numerous friends of the deceased.

On arrival at the Cathedral of the Holy Trinity, the cortege was met by the officiating clergy. A large congregation took part in the impressive service. The Dead March from Saul was played by the organist at the conclusion of the service.

All premises in Main Street were closed and route was lined with sympathetic onlookers. Revenue Inspectors carried the coffin to the grave at the cemetery at North Front.

The principle mourners were Mrs Bethell and Mrs Wilson Smith, who were accompanied by Mrs Brooks and Lady Robertson: His Excellency the Acting Governor and Commander in Chief Brigadier W. T. Brooks.

Mrs Bethell desires to thank those who have by letters, cards and wreaths and in other ways shown their sympathy in her bereavement. She would like to thank those who attended the service in the Cathedral and at the Cemetery as well as those who closed their premises during the funeral, and would ask all to accept this notice as a heartfelt appreciation of the many kind expressions of sympathy which she has received.

There is no mention of The Hon. D.L. Bethell's three sons, who, it must be assumed, did not attend the funeral.

Stoke Newington, London March 2024

Dear Dad,

I have tried to imagine what it was like for you when your father committed suicide in Gibraltar. I have taken some liberties. I have had to. You never spoke about it even when Robin, my brother and your son, committed suicide. Had I bothered to ask, which I didn't, as I too was heavily into avoidance when it came to excavating the intimate substrata of our family history, I suspect, you would have blocked that experience too. I know that it is quite common for people to blank out memories of traumatic events in their life. It's called Dissociative Amnesia[6]

If you had by some aberration broken your silence, I am sure you would have told me that your primary response was to look after your mother. After all, her husband's suicide destroyed her life. You boys were all she had. It is not hard to understand how traumatic it was for her and I imagine you had to stand in for your father. You were fourteen. It must have been a hell of a responsibility. And then there were the financial implications.

[6.] Dissociative Amnesia occurs when a person blocks out certain information, often associated with a stressful or traumatic event, leaving the person unable to remember important personal information. It has been linked to overwhelming stress, which may be caused by traumatic events such as war, abuse, accidents, or suicide.

You must have thought that you would have to leave Sherborne as up to that point your fees had been paid by the Colonial Service. But I know that you were lucky. Your housemaster arranged for your fees to be paid by the school. I looked it up in the school archives. Under a section describing School Fees Remission it says: 1935 'D.A.D.J. Bethell (d) and brother R.A Bethell – their father was Colonial Treasurer at Gibraltar and died from a self-inflicted wound, probably due to severe nerve strain in WW1.' Do you think he was under severe strain due to his time on the front? Did he seem disturbed to you? His medical records suggest that his wounds were superficial and he made a full recovery. There is no mention of shell shock.

He had rapidly climbed up the ranks of the Colonial Service with no suggestion of an unstable mind. The evidence I have found suggests he was a popular and successful role model for you. He should have been at ease with himself. And yet I also know that the impact of the First World War on the survivors took many forms and there were many examples of delayed, what we would now call, Post Traumatic Stress. Yet, how would you know? You did not see that much of him did you. I mean it was just the summer holidays and even then, he was out most of the time, either at the office or pursuing his hobbies or socialising

I wonder whether you did try to understand why he did it? Did your mother ever discuss it with you? From what I remember, her strong sense of social propriety and her pride would not have allowed her to open up even to her friends, let alone her children. But you must have wondered. I think your brother Denis suggested that it was gambling debts. I know that your father was a keen race-goer. Could he have got himself into trouble that way? It would be strange for a professional accountant to get into money problems. Strange but not impossible. We know that gambling can be addictive and that social embarrassment was a terrifying prospect that had driven many of his class to suicide.

I think I have now learnt that talking about those things does help. But for too long I lined up with you. I did not speak or even think too much about Robin, your son, who committed suicide at the age of thirty. Instead focussed on his sons, my nephews. But looking back, I am distressed by the way I avoided the subject. I wish we had spoken about it. Especially if you had been prepared to talk about your father's death and how it had made you feel. That would have been the basis for a very different relationship and once again I feel an opportunity lost.

Now I need to think about what it was like when you got back to school. I am of course familiar with your school because you arranged for it to be my school. And to be honest I don't think it had changed much in twenty-five years. But it will be hard to imagine the inside of your house because you could not enter another boy's house. As a result, Harper House is a bit of a closed book to me. But I am not so interested in the physical geography of the place but rather the emotional climate. How would your fellow pupils react to the news that your father had killed himself? If my own experience is anything to go by, denial was the guiding strategy for dealing with 'emotional stuff'. And that causes me to wonder what happens to the shock, grief and massive burden of responsibility when there is no one to share it with and no responsible adult to turn to.

Love

Hum

In Love And War

CHAPTER 9

Back to School

Harper House, Sherborne School. September 1935

It is the beginning of term and Drew has been summoned to see his house master, Mr Barlow. He knocks on the study door.

-Come! Ah, Bethell. Good to see you. Had a decent trip back?

-Very decent thanks, sir.

-We were very sorry to hear about your father. A sad business. Very sad. How's your mother? Holding up?

-Yes sir. Holding up.

-Well it's going to be a bit of a change for her isn't it. She has been in touch. Was very worried about the fees. I told her I would put in a special request for fee remission, and I am very glad to say that all is well. You don't have to worry about that. Your mother doesn't have to worry about that at least. Should cover the fees until you leave. That'll be 1939 for you Drew. And we're paying for Tony too when he gets here

-Thank you, sir.

-What about you? Must have been a bit of a shock. Quite a few boys in the house have lost their fathers. You are not alone. Most of them through divorce which is a bit different I suppose. But losing your father is not easy. Not easy at all. Especially when . . . you know. By his own hand as they say. Difficult very difficult.

-Yes, sir.

-Of course, it's best not to brood on it. Brooding doesn't help.

-No sir.

-Good man. Keep active that's the ticket. Takes your mind off things.

-Rugger, sir?

-Not your strong suit, I know that. But the OCT. You're doing well. Make you a sergeant soon. Bound to. (*There is a long pause*) Any questions?

-Well sir, I was wondering . . . I'm just not sure.

-What are you not sure about?

-What should I say to the others? The boys. What do I tell them? I haven't said anything yet. Should I tell the others. The teachers. The prefects. Do they need to know what happened?

-No, I think not. I'm not sure the chaps would understand. We don't want them ribbing you. I always think it is best to keep the personal family stuff to oneself. I mean you could tell a few of your close chums that your old man has passed away. No details of course. But tell' em to keep it to themselves. Don't spread it around. Teachers don't need to know. As long as you can cope, and there's no blubbing in lessons.

-No blubbing sir. Never. (*Pause*) My father was important. In Gibraltar. He had a huge funeral. Closed off the streets. We weren't allowed to go, but we heard about it.

-I'm sure he was. And of course, he was a war hero too. Wounded in action. Always takes its toll of course. Too many men still suffering the effects of that dreadful show. Quite a few find it all too hard and end it all.

-Our father didn't suffer from the war, sir. He was fighting fit.

- Physically of course. Fine figure of a man. I remember him well. Came to your first Commem. But the mind gets damaged too you know. Often can't tell what's happening up there.

-Yes sir.

-Right, run along. Almost time for lunch. I think its shepherd's pie followed by spotted dick and custard. My favourite.

-Mine too, sir. Thank you, sir.

CHAPTER 10

School Fees

Harper House, Sherborne School. August 1935

Application for reduction in fees for a boy already at the school and for a younger brother who wishes to enter.

Application is made that a possible reduction in fees should be made in the case of D.A.D.J. Bethell of Harper House, and in the case of his younger brother who is entered to come into this house either in January 1936 or in May 1936.

The elder boy is now aged 14 years 10 months, the younger is aged 13 years. In July last the boys' father, who was Colonial Treasurer at Gibraltar, died from a self-inflicted wound. It was thought this was due to extreme nerve strain as a result of the Great War, followed by life in tropical climates. Mr Bethell served throughout the Great War. After this he was given among other positions in the Colonial Service a *post in British Somaliland where he served for some years. In an unusually short time he had risen to the position which he held at his death. He left a widow and three sons- the boys mentioned above and a third aged 18 months.*

Mrs Bethell now finds herself hard put to it to bring up and educate three boys. She has formed a high opinion of Sherborne and wishes to do all in her power to keep the elder boy here and send the second here also. She has no relatives who can give her financial help. She receives a pension in respect of her husband from the government. She has also applied to and obtained funds from the Trustees of the Sarawak Fund. Beside these assets there is also a capital sum bringing in annual interest of £60 until the second son reaches the age of 18.

The total per annum income available to her is therefore as follows:

From pension.	*£339.*	*11s*	*4d*
From Sarawak Fund	*£75*		
From interest on capital	*£60*		
Total.	*£474.*	*11s*	*4d*

It is hoped that a reduction to half-fees may be made in Tuition for the elder boy and that this reduction may be retrospective in respect of the past summer term. The last clause is requested because Mrs Bethell has incurred very considerable expense in moving during the summer holidays from Gibraltar to England. It is also hoped that the second son may be allowed to enter the school on half fees. In the case of both boys, half fees for Boarding have already been offered, and in the case of the elder boy granted.

It is thought that this is a very deserving case both from the record of Mr Bethell and also from the record of the elder bson while he has been at Sherborne. This boy came to the school in 1934. On entry he was placed in Form II; he has risen from this for to Form IVa (a rise of four forms in three terms). His record in the house has been exemplary and a most favourable report can be given on his character and promise. Beside this he has represented his house in Junior events in Football and Swimming. The younger boy has as great promise as the elder, being at present senior boy at his Preparatory School. He will be about one month too old to take the scholarship examination next June, though in fact it is not thought he would prove good enough to gain a scholarship.

It is hoped that both boys will go in the Colonial Service, the intention being to use the capital sum mentioned above for further education at the University with the possible help of Kitchener Scholarships.

I ask for your prompt consideration of this matter.

Yours faithfully

R.M.M. BARLOW

Housemaster Harper House.

Stoke Newington, London March 2024

Dear Dad,

By all accounts Barlow was a lot more sympathetic than I have made him out. After all he went out of his way to secure half fees for you and Tony. And had already reduced your boarding costs. Perhaps I have laid on the caricature a bit thick. And yet, twenty-five years later I had a housemaster who was considered to be 'good with the boys', and I am afraid I can hear every word of my Barlow coming from him. I recall sessions in his study when I was very vulnerable and homesick and his pep talks were in the same vein.

I find it hard to believe that there was anybody to talk to. I also feel confident that your father's suicide was never mentioned and you were advised not to make too much of a fuss.

I have in front of me the house photo for Harper House in 1935. You are in the back row with a long thin face that I don't recognise. You have a fine head of dark hair. You are clearly tall for your age. You rather stand out from the boys on either side. You do look at ease with yourself. Of course, this will have been taken in early July. Shortly after this picture was taken you would have taken the train down to Southampton to board the P&O liner that would take you to Gibraltar for the start of your summer holidays. By the end of the month your father would be dead.

It occurs to me now that the scene I invented in Barlow's study would have happened at least a month after your father died. I have a huge hole in your narrative. What was it like in the aftermath? The letter requesting your fee remission suggests your mother come back on the boat with you, having closed up Beaulieu House? Were you already the man of the house? Perhaps that is where you developed the trait which you subsequently used to manage any family crisis: you went into organisational mode. I remember that you kicked into action when your son killed himself. No time for grieving: your emotional energy was diverted into administration. In Gibraltar you would have been burying your feelings in a frantic attempt to deflect your mother's grief. And I can recognise that. When Robin died my mother, your wife, was ravaged with a primal grief. I had to deflect that grief through platitudes and distraction. To survive I had to bury my grief and it took forty years to disinter my feeling of both love and loss. Did that happen to you? As we have seen, you have a strong emotional life. When it came to wooing my mother, you poured out your feelings. But when it came to the trauma of your father's death and the harsh realities of your war, you could not break with the habits you could have learnt while clearing out Beulieu House and escorting your mother home to her newly impoverished future.

I also have the Harper House photo for 1937. Two years after your father's suicide. You haven't changed a lot. You are still in the back row: you still seem to be amongst the 'other ranks'. I would have liked to know more about your school days: about the years after your father died. I have trawled the Sherborne School archives but all that I can find are fragments. Snippets that offer some clues but little detail. It seems that you were more confident in yourself than I ever was at that age. You were a conformist and I want you to have fulfilled the promise suggested by Barlow's assessment of you as he was selling you to the grants committee:

His record in the house has been exemplary and a most favourable report can be given on his character and promise.

And it looks as if you did not let the death of your father jeopardise that promise.

Love

Hum

In Love And War

CHAPTER 11

School Fragments

Sherborne School, Dorset, 1935-39

There is very little documentation about the years after Drew Bethell's father committed suicide. However, in a list of Harper House Distinctions for Michaelmas Term in 1935 it shows *Hutchinson D.: Head of the Day Room and Bethell D.A.D.J.: Head Fag.* The Day Room at Sherborne was where boys spent their first four or five terms before graduating to a shared study. The Head of the Dayroom was an honour bestowed on the boy most likely to keep some order in the harsh environment where some thirty feral young teenage boys would congregate when not in lessons, on the playing field or in bed. The younger boys would be the fags: on call at all times to act as menial servants to the older boys in their studies. Whilst still reeling from the suicide of his father, it would seem my father was the one who had to work out rotas and make sure his charges fulfilled their obligations to the older boys: making toast, running to the tuck shop and taking dirty games kit to the laundry.

I would have assumed that the next term, Bethell D A D J ought to have been in the running for Head of Dayroom, but to my dismay I see on the list of Distinctions for the Lent Term 1936, that Bethell D.A.D.J is still Head Fag. And one *Gray A.M.* is *Head of Dayroom*. I feel there was some injustice here and that my father lacked the assertiveness to make his case for the top job.

I can write authoritatively about this system as it had not changed one iota some thirty years later when I attended Sherborne. I too failed to make the top job in the Day Room, but nor was I Head Fag. What I do remember is waiting for the electric bell above the door to ring which was the sign for four or five of us to race to the study where the lazy senior boy would be waiting ready to allocate whatever demeaning task was on offer to the last one to arrive at his door. Speed was of the essence and I feel my father would have got there first and avoided some of the more tedious tasks.

Bethell D.A.D.J. disappears from the archive for the next few years. The next time I see him, he is going fishing. This from the Harper House Record of Activities:

May 22nd 1937

Constant and Bethell: went fishing in a stream near Marston Magna. It rained most of the eight miles there, but we assembled our rods and set to work, Constant's had a worm and Bethell a fly spoon. Bethell saw a trout try to climb the concrete slope, but as they started to fish the pool, the miller who owned the weir told us to remove ourselves. *The miller's name is Anstey. Then we went further upstream and fished one rise, but it was late so we came back. It poured all the way back.*

D.A. Bethell

He was an enthusiastic fly fisherman for most of his life and here he is already pursuing that interest. They do not seem to have caught anything, but the encounter with the stroppy miller makes for a good story to take back to school.

I then catch up with him in 1938 at a meeting of the Harper House Literary Society. The minutes read as follows:

On Sunday March 19th the society met for the last meeting of the term. D.A.D.J. Bethell read a paper on 'Gibraltar'.

The reader commenced with a brief historical sketch commenting on the strategic importance and the invincibility of the Rock, but the main body of the paper was contained in his recollections of the life of Gibraltar.

I am on the edge of my seat. What will he say about Gibraltar life? Will he mention his father? What about life in Beaulieu House? As far as the minutes go, he will do no such thing. It is two and half years since his father died. He has ploughed on with his adolescent life. He will be reminded of those fraught days when he sees his mother in the holidays, but even between the two of them, there will be a vow of silence. The minute-taker continues:

He spoke about its natural features, its inhabitants and their customs. The paper was vivid and forceful. There were some stylistic defects and a certain informality of expression.

I have school reports which say almost the same about my literary efforts: a forceful writer with a certain informality of expression. As I have said before, we reproduce more than we transform.

But the result, whatever its literary merits was an original and entertaining study. The discussion that followed was primarily concerned with Gibraltar as a strategic port, perhaps because of the European crisis. It indicated that the reader's subject was one of general interest whilst once again the society received the benefit of a first-hand knowledge of the evening's topic.

The week before the society held its meeting on 12th March 1938, Hitler had marched his forces into Austria and been greeted by cheering crowds. It was the start of the Anschluss. The day after the society heard about the strategic importance of Gibraltar, the Gun Laws in Nazi Germany were amended to ban Jewish gun merchants.

Then I get sight of the class lists for Summer term 1939, where I find a list of boys in the Army Class. It seems that boys who expressed an inclination for the military life were grouped together. They were directed towards a more practical set of subjects as opposed to the majority who would have focussed on the classics and the humanities.

His academic endeavours are listed as follows.

ARMY CLASS 1939
Sixth Year
Bethell D A D J.   E1 P1 C1   M1 F1

So, he was studying English, Physics, Chemistry, French and Maths. He is in the top set in each subject and it is indeed a practical selection that will play into his future career. Physics will help him to understand the parabola of an artillery shell, Chemistry will lead to an understanding of the chemical components of an explosive charge, Maths will also be handy as he calculates the logistics of an artillery barrage and French will help him engage with the locals as his regiment retreats through Belgium to the beaches of Dunkirk. I am struck by the contrast with my own three A levels taken at the same age at the same school in 1966: English, History and French. Just three subjects, none of which were of much practical use. I imagine that those not in the Army class would have had a restricted selection more in line with the great divide between arts and science.

Finally, I come across the brief summary of his school career. It reads:

> Came 1934, Captain of Swimming, Trebles (1936-37-38-39), 2nd XV, Gym Squad 1938-39, Sergeant in the OTC, PT Instructor with Badge, School Fencing, Member of the Agriculturalists to RMA Woolwich.

I am not sure I recognise this young man. It took me a while to discover what he had achieved with his 'Trebles' for four successive years. It turns out you achieved a Treble when you could 'swim 400 yards in 10 minutes or other hard tests' so clearly an accomplished swimmer from an early age and not surprisingly made Captain of the Swimming Team. I have to say I rarely saw him immerse himself in water. I understood that a war-time incident had irreparably damaged his ear drums and he could not risk getting water in his ears.

Sherborne was a school that prioritised physical activity often over intellectual prowess. The gym squad put on faintly fascistic displays in the school quad and my father was clearly a willing participant. There is a photo of the school gym squad and again he looks like he fits in well. There is a steely resolve about his expression.

It does not surprise me that he was a Sergeant in the Officer Training Corps. He was clearly destined for the army. All five hundred boys were in the OTC. There is an extraordinary picture of the entire school in serried ranks, dressed in uniforms which I must assume were left over from the First World War (when I was in what was later called the CCF we had uniforms and uniforms left over from the Second World War). It was the Officer Training Corps: none of these privileged young men would ever end up amongst the Other Ranks, and as a Sergeant my father would have been learning the basics of military leadership.

For a while I was baffled by his membership of *The Agriculturalists*. To my knowledge he never took the slightest interest in horticulture throughout his life. A little research revealed that *The Agriculturalists* was actually a cricket club which played matches against the local village teams. An article in the school magazine at the time explains:

> Cricket must be played seriously and the fine arts developed if it is to be fully enjoyed. This is true enough for those who can appreciate and practice these fine arts. But there are many who, lacking this ability, find pleasure in the ruder elements of cricket. The Agriculturalist Cricket Club has been formed to cater for the weaker cricket players who have little opportunity in school games.

I am relieved. This makes perfect sense. My father was not interested in cricket and I cannot remember a single conversation about either a county or the national cricket team as I was growing up. As for me, my skills on the cricket field (we all had to play at least four times a week) tended towards the agricultural whilst at Sherborne and I only developed an interest in the performance of others much later in life. I did manage to get hold of *The Agriculturalists'* fixture list for 1939 and it seems that they played their last fixture on July 28th against the village of Yetminister, where my mother lived for twenty years after my father's death.

Finally, his destination: *the RMA (Royal Military Academy) Woolwich*. If you wanted to join an infantry or cavalry regiment you went to the RMA Sandhurst, but if you wanted to join the Royal Artillery you went to Woolwich, the home of the Gunners. What this paltry record does not show is that he received a Kitchener Scholarship to attend the Academy. He began there in August 1939, but he had barely started the two-year course when war was declared and he was transferred to an Officer

Cadet Training Unit. This was a fast-track officer training programme which took just five months before graduates were shipped off to war. In my father's case he began in September and by January 1940, still aged only 18 he was passed ready for war and joined the 19th Field Regiment. The regiment was supporting the Kings Shropshire Light Infantry based near the commune of Cysoing, fifteen kilometres east of Lille on the border with Belgium. Then his regiment moved further into Belgium until May 10th when the Germans invaded neutral Holland and Belgium. Within days they were retreating, a frenetic withdrawal that ended on the beaches of Dunkirk.

1935-1939

D. A D.J. Bethell (Centre) Captain of Sherborne School Swimming Team 1939.

Stoke Newington, London April 2024

Dear Dad,

So that's the best I can do when it comes to your school days. As ever, it makes me even more frustrated that I never spoke to you about that time. We went to the same school! Some of my teachers taught you; there was lots to talk about and yet we never did. I would have loved to hear you reminisce about those days. I can see you now, sitting in the cabin of your yacht, with a glass of Calvados in your hand and I am sitting opposite you. The cabin is warm and the conditions are ideal for a trip back to Harper House and the fishing expedition to Marston Magna. I would ask you about how you became such a good swimmer. Did you know there was a war looming? Did you think it would involve you? Did you look forward to the prospect? And after another glass of Calvados I might have risked a question about your time in Gibraltar, perhaps using your paper to the Literary Society as a way in. But, although I spent many evenings in that cabin and drank many glasses of cheap spirits, we never got anywhere close to what matters to me as I sit here now, ten years older than you when you died, digging into your past and yearning to know more. But of course, it is just too late.

As I said, you did not seem to be a high flier but nor were you a failure. Within the expectations of the time, I suspect you were better prepared for the rigours of war than I would have been. You were certainly physically prepared: a fine swimmer and a gymnast. I know that you had inherited some of the charm that made your father such a player in 1930s Gibraltar. The army class gave you a grounding in the practical subjects that would have stood you in good stead at the Gunnery Officer Cadet Training Unit.

Of course, I am particularly interested in your emotional resilience. I am assuming that having to keep a stiff upper lip when it came to your father's suicide taught you to build a protective layer around your vulnerabilities and your fears. You must have had them, but as you said to me: "One was taught not to talk about oneself".

It feels that I am leaving your school days unresolved, despite my best efforts in the Sherborne archive. But it is time to move on. It's wartime and I left you on the train from Margate with your mouth still sore but perhaps revived with a mug of nourishing soup. But then I lose you. I am not going to see you again for more than two years and the only hard evidence I have comes from a newspaper clipping I found in your mother's papers. She only kept the first page so there are some tantalising details missing. However, under the headline **19th Fd. Regt. Guns were Hun's Nightmare**, the article describes the retreat from Dunkirk, and then goes on:

> Two rather disheartening years followed, the regiment

> being milked of specialists and trained personnel to reinforce units overseas and then, at last, orders came to embark for North Africa in support of battalions of the Grenadiers and Irish Guards of the 24th Guards Brigade.

It does not seem that you were either specialist or trained enough to have been 'milked off' to another unit, and I have no way of knowing whether you were disheartened by those two years in limbo. What is certain is that you were fully recovered when I catch up with you in March 1943. You are in Tunisia and you are based in the town of Medjez el Bab where you are supporting First Battalion, the Irish Guard in the final months of the North Africa campaign. After El Alamein, the Germans under Rommel were being pushed back into the Tunis peninsular, but he was not giving up and had fortified a number of defensive positions on high ground. These needed to be taken before the 8th Army and US allies could push the Germans out of Africa.

You have seen very little action since Dunkirk, but according to the regimental records on Monday 29th March:

> Preparations made for support attack by 2 Company Irish Guards 96/97 Battery moved to forward positions.

96/97 was your battery and you were trained as a Forward Observation Officer (F.O.O). The Irish Guards have been given orders to attack a well defended mountainous ridge, known to the British as Recce Ridge. The regimental record for the following day is brief:

> Supported attack by 2 Coy Irish Guards at 0600 with 65-minute task table. 96/97 Battery fired smoke screen during time of main attack. F.O.O. Captain D.A. D.J. Bethell reported wounded, failed to return. Two signallers missing.

There is very little else to help me understand exactly what happened to you but I do have testimony from the Irish Guards to help me picture the scene. So, as with my fictional efforts to imagine your time on the beaches outside Dunkirk, I am going to accompany you and try to imagine just what happened and what it felt like.

Love

Hum.

In Love And War

CHAPTER 12

Captured on Recce Ridge

Outside Medjez El Bab, Tunisia. 29/30th March 1943

It almost midnight and it is cold. This may be the edge of the Sahara Desert, but it gets cold at night. You might expect ten or eleven degrees, but tonight certainly feels colder. There was rain a few days ago heavy enough to turn the tracks into mud, but during the day the sun dried up the landscape. It is a clear night and there is a panoply of bright stars. There is a low moon, just a quarter that does not make it any easier to see. There is a group of around a hundred men coming towards me, marching four a breast. There is a relaxed parade-ground order to their progress. This is 2 Company of the 1st Battalion the Irish Guards. They are mere silhouettes and yet I can tell they are dressed for battle. They wear the distinctive British Brodie Mark 2 helmets and they are encumbered with weapons protruding. Rifles pointing upwards off the shoulder and a few Bren guns strapped across the back. They are silent but their boots are in step, a light crunching rhythm on the sandy track. They pass me by.

They have had their orders They are on their way to Recce Ridge - a desolate rocky outcrop a mile to the north of Medjez el Bab. They know that there the German position has been reinforced to protect the supply lines for Rommel's last-ditch defence of Tunis. The orders are for 2 Company to make *'a probing attack'* and *'kill or capture all enemy in the area'* which meant, as was written up in the Company Orders, *'advancing across the valley in the dark, climbing the mined slopes, a quick in-and-out battle on the ridge and then a withdrawal in daylight back across the valley'*. The orders came from Central Command 1st Army based well behind the action and the simplicity of the phrase 'probing attack' and the idea of 'a quick in-and-out battle' somewhat belied the challenge and the risks on the ground. Central Command were not aware that the Germans had been expecting an attack for over two weeks and had been digging themselves into the shelter of the crags and gullies on the summit of the ridge.

It is just past midnight and they are on their way. I am walking with my father. He is now twenty-two years old and has three pips on his battle dress to denote his recent promotion to Captain. He has a set of binoculars slung over one shoulder and a map case hanging from the other. He has an Enfield Mark 2 revolver in a holster on his belt. He has two signallers walking behind him. They carry the heavy radio as well as cables and a telescopic aerial. When the time comes they will set up a Forward Observation Post. My father will be able to hear the Irish Guards Company Commander Major Sam Bucknill as well as send information back to his battery of guns that will deliver a barrage of 25-pound shells onto the German positions at the top of the ridge.

As they leave the outskirts of the town, they pass a tent with an open front. In it stand two more signallers with their radios set out on a table. This will be the local control centre. The Company have a few hours to get in position for the attack which is scheduled for 0530 hours as dawn breaks. At that point the battalion commander, Colonel Scott, will be watching and listening as his men go into battle and with any luck return unscathed. It is after all a 'quick in and out' operation.

My father and the three platoons of 2 Company are well on their way to the base of the ridge. They are walking at a brisk pace. My father has no trouble keeping up: he was a brisk walker even in his sixties. I, on the other hand, am feeling my seventy-five years. I am breathing hard and I am carrying nothing but my ethereal curiosity and a lurking anxiety as to how this will play out for these men whose apparently simple task is to 'capture or kill as many of the enemy' as possible. There is a cold wind that blows down from the ridge. It will be chilly once they are in position waiting for the dawn but now they are keeping warm as they stride on. Spirits are high. This is the first time they have gone into battle since both units arrived from the UK just two weeks ago on the 14th March 1943.

They have now crossed the Beja Road and the formation has broken up as they make their way over the broken ground. There are no more sandy tracks, now they are having to make their way over unstable rocks and sharply aggressive shrub. They need to be silent, but I can hear whispered curses as boots get caught and balance is lost. My father is light on his feet but his signallers are carrying forty pounds of equipment and keeping balance is harder for them. And as for me, my balance is hopeless and I could use his steadying arm. But he has no time or inclination to help his as yet unborn son. He must keep up with his Irish comrades as they make their way towards the ridge which is now looming above them, an evil exoskeletal shape against the clear night sky.

The sloping approach is getting steeper and progress is slowing. It is 0230. There is still plenty of time to make it into position just below the crest of the ridge ready for the planned attack. What makes progress even slower is that a previous recce, the day before, had established that the steeper face of the ridge had been mined. No one is sure how prevalent the mines are but there is a need for eternal vigilance. The S-Mine was deadly if you stepped on the protruding rod. But the terrain on Recce Ridge was so rocky there were only a few locations with enough soil to bury a mine. If you kept your feet on rock you were safe. I keep a close eye on my father's boots. I cannot afford for him to die on this night.

As the face of the ridge gets steeper and rocks larger, progress is slow. Silence was the rule but if you got close to Corporal Fildes, the 2 Company signaller, every few minutes you can hear him whisper a 'tuning call' "Paddy two. . . Paddy two". This is picked up back at base and will reassure Colonel Scott, who by this time is in the control tent, that all is well. So far.

After two hours of slow progress, suddenly, the head of the column drops out of sight. "Patrol" The word is hissed and urgent, and passes across the group. No one needs telling twice.

Men drop to the ground and freeze. My father drops and I notice that one of his signallers has slipped and seems to crash to the ground. My father puts out a reassuring hand. Neither he nor I can see anything, but there is a faint clinking and I think I can hear a German command. No one moves. Discovery now will jeopardise the whole mission. I am waiting for the alarm to be raised, for the shooting to start. But my father seems calm. He is only twenty-two and yet he is taking the alarming tension in his stride. I am in awe. It seems that the patrol is more than a hundred yards away and they head along the ridge, away from us. I am relieved.

By 0430 hours the Company is in position about two hundred yards below the ridge. My father is still with the main company. His signallers have caught up with him and are sitting by him breathing heavily. My father has made his way across to where Major Bucknill is sitting with his signaller who has his set open and tuned. As he approaches, he hears the Major make contact with his Colonel back in the control tent.

"No trouble so far. We dodged a patrol on the way over. We are more than halfway up the slope and have been for some time. It is much steeper from now on. We'll start climbing again in a few minutes. Have the guns got one up the spout? So long. Over."

"All set here. Good luck, Sam. Off"

My father reassures him that the guns of 96/97 battery do indeed have shells up the spout, but now is the time for him to separate from the Company and find a position from where he can observe the action and call up artillery as and when it is needed.

"Sir, I would like to move to the right and get up onto that rocky outcrop to set up my F.O.P. It is just below the crest and it should be a good place to see you. Do I have permission to move?"

"I imagine the enemy will be concentrated on the central section. You should be safe up there. Let me know when you are in position. We'll be moving at 0530 and we'll need cover before then."

"And you shall have it, sir."

My father and his signallers set off, scrambling over the scree. I can see the rocky outcrop he is aiming for. It looks pretty damned exposed to me. Does he really need to be that far up? If it were up to me I would have found somewhere lower down the slope, less exposed. But it is not up to me, a cautious seventy-six-year-old who knows how things will play out once daylight comes to Recce Ridge on the morning of the 30th March 1943. But my father is an enthusiast, he always has been, and this is his first chance to show his observer skills in a battle situation. He knows that it is risky, but if he has a good view he can direct the gunfire more accurately. He can provide Major Bicknill and his men with an accurate barrage that will keep German heads down as they advance up the ridge and 'capture and kill the enemy'.

He is stopping now and encourages the signallers to do the same. It is still dark and the quarter moon has long since dropped below the horizon, but a silhouette would still be visible against the starlit sky. The rocks are increasingly chaotic and unpredictable. He is making slow progress and the signallers are making heavy weather and I know what it is like to climb at night. I have done so in Snowdonia. I know about false summits. I know how your objective never seems to get closer. But I have never had to keep my back low and my profile hidden from an enemy above me. I have never had to manage the fear of making a sound that could alert the enemy. A slip, a ricochet curse as my binocular case slaps against an errant piece of sandstone. But my father is on a mission and he will not be deterred by my elderly caution. The clock is ticking. It is well past 0430 and my father needs to be in position in good time. There is a glow in the sky to the east - a mix of the darkest purple and soft orange hue. Dawn is approaching along the Mediterranean ready to come up like thunder on the rocky hills of Tunisia.

Even though I have fallen behind and am observing from below, I see that my father and his small team have made it to the rocky outcrop. The signallers are preparing the radio. An aerial has been laid out across the rocks. It must not stick up into the lightening sky. My father has positioned himself on an outcrop, he is visible but it is a risk he must take if he is to see as much as possible of the battle zone. The binoculars are out and his map is on his lap. I know that as well as a map he has a Fire Plan for the morning. This is a grid showing what each barrage will consist of. I have it in front of me here on my desk but it makes no sense to me. Under Rate of Fire is written:

Zero to Plus 3 -Intense. Plus 3 to Plus 35 – Normal.
but first minute on each task- Intense.

All I can say is it looks as if the fire power my father can bring down on the ridge will be intense.

Just before 0500 there is a burst of machine gun fire, followed by sporadic rifle shots. Then the crump of several mortars. The radio comes alive. It is Major Bucknill.

"I need artillery cover. Heavy as you can make it. Concentrate on the eastern edge of the ridge".

Dawn has broken and my father can see to confirm the grid references on the map and takes over the mic to call back to his battery. He does not have to say much. He orders up the first fifteen minutes of intense fire. And within seconds the first shells are flying through the air and landing on the crest of the ridge. They come in bursts of ten and my father can see the white impact smoke fly into the air, moments before the earsplitting crump reaches him. An earth-raising cacophony which you feel through the soles of your boots. A thunderous rolling sound that is bad enough to hear from a distance but surely shattering to those manning the defensive fox holes. As each barrage lands my father can confirm the accuracy. If a barrage dropped short, I can hear him call for a correction. After fifteen minutes some two hundred shells have exploded on the ridge, which is now covered in thick dust. Silence falls, but not for long. From the slope below the ridge, I can hear small arms fire. I am no expert but my father will be able to recognise the crack of the Lee Enfield rifles, the staccato snapping of the Bren guns, and more ominously the hysterical whirring sound of the Spandau machine guns firing off 500 rounds per minute.

I am familiar with the expression 'the fog of war'. And standing close to my father as he waits and listens as 2 Company attack Recce Ridge, I come to realise just how frustrating and confusing so much of active warfare is to experience. There is clearly a battle raging. 2 Company are in the thick of it. It is not yet full daylight but there is enough light to look across the ridge. It is possible to make out figures emerging from the dust, but as the intensity of small arms fire increases, it is impossible to make out who is making progress, who is being pushed back, who is doing the killing and who is doing the dying. There are wounded men amongst the rocks, that is for sure. You can hear men shouting in the brief gaps between the relentless whirring of the Spandau machine guns. It is possible to make out men running and scrambling for cover. The Irish Guards are exposed. They are being pushed back. My father could retreat but he does not. I want him to cut his losses. He facilitated that awesome barrage that should have subdued the German defenders. He could go and perhaps he is thinking that he will, when the radio crackles into life. It is Major Bicknill. He is no longer sounding relaxed. There is a desperation in his voice as he calls for a barrage of smoke shells to provide cover for his men's withdrawal. The signaller switches band to put my father in contact with his batteries. He wants smoke and he wants it now. There is an ominous pause and then a whir as the shells pass over head. They hit the face of the ridge, smoke belches out and the whole area disappears into billowing foul-smelling clouds of smoke . For a while the smoke quietens the gunfire. As it clears I can make out men clambering down through the rocks. But there are fewer, far fewer than there were when we left them at the start.

It is hard to understand quite what has happened. The Irish Guards are in retreat but my father is still at his post As the signallers pack their gear and my father is looking through his binoculars trying to work out just where he should go, there is an almighty explosion. A *Stielhandgranate*, the German stick grenade, has landed between my father and his signallers. It throws him off his rock and he is smashed to the ground. His helmet saves his head but he is stunned. His binoculars are crushed into his chest. As he comes too, he feels a stab of pain in his shoulder where a piece of shrapnel has embedded itself. When some sense eventually returns, he sees that both signallers have taken the blast. They lie comatose. One has blood oozing from his elbow. He feels he should go to help. To check on his men. But he is still reeling and there is a violent ringing in his ears. Sounds are muffled and distorted. He can only hear the cacophony reverberating around his skull. And that is a pity because he does not hear the sound of the *Oberfeldwebel* who is standing over him with a rifle pointing at his head. When he does turn towards the indistinct rumble of another voice, the situation is startling and then shocking. He is about to be captured. He is to be a prisoner. He is in no fit state to make an escape. He turns towards the signallers and finds that two other Germans are leaning over both men, but there is no sign of life. He has lost his men and lost his freedom. And it seems that he has lost his hearing as well. I know that the blast from that grenade has wrecked his ear drums.

I am hiding behind a rock. I am well away from the action. I have been able to reconstruct a plausible version of what happens up to this point from various regimental records and personal accounts from those who were there, but once again I have lost sight of my father. I have found the testimony of a German deserter who told the Irish Guards Intelligence Officer that by 1000 hours on the morning 30th March, 50 British prisoners were taken to the village of Toukabeur about five miles north of Recce Ridge on the German side and 'with them were two Royal Artillery Captains'. One of those two was almost certainly my father. I know that at some point he was handed over to the Italians and shipped back to Italy where he ended up in PG 49, an Italian POW camp in Fontanellato on the Piedmont Plain, South of Parma. I will catch up with him there. He is reported as Wounded and Missing by the British War Office Casualty Branch. I do know that he was very hard of hearing throughout his life and there is some indication that the grenade blast on Recce Ridge had done permanent damage to his ear drums.

The battle for Recce Ridge on the morning of Monday 30th March 1943 was a calamity for my father but a catastrophe for 2 Company of the First Battalion of the Irish Guards. It will go down in regimental history as one of the worst engagements of their war. Of the 103 officers and men who set out from Medjez El Bab at midnight, only seven made it back and three of them were wounded. The rest were either killed, badly wounded or taken prisoner. Major Sam Bicknill was amongst the dead. He had married his wife Olivia on 21st January 1943 whilst on leave before embarking for North Africa.

Lance Corporal John Kenneally was in No 1 Company and did not take part in the action on Recce Ridge, but he observed it and later wrote:

> *As ordinary infantry soldiers, by the very nature of things, we were not privy to the 'Grand Design'. We had to do as ordered and follow the man in front - very much a case of 'Ours is not to reason why, etc'. I suspect our battalion officers were in a similar position, but the powers-that-be threw No 2 Company's lives away. As was said in the First World War, 'It was not the Germans who took our lives, it was our own Generals who did for us.'*

Exactly a month later John Kenneally was awarded the Victoria Cross for extreme bravery in the face of the enemy on a mountain ridge at Jebel Bou Aoukaz just fifteen miles north of Recce Ridge.

CHAPTER 13

Mrs Bethell waits for news

Bishops Down Court, Kent. April 1943

```
Tel. No.: Liverpool Wavertree 4000.                    THE WAR OFFICE,
Any further communication on this subject              CASUALTY BRANCH,
should be addressed to :—                              BLUE COAT SCHOOL,
    The Under Secretary of State,                      CHURCH ROAD,
    The War Office,                                    WAVERTREE,
        Casualty Branch,                               LIVERPOOL 15.
        Blue Coat School,
            Church Road, Wavertree,
                Liverpool 15.                          10th April, 1943.
and the following number quoted :
Our Ref./OS.134.B.    (Casualties)
Your Ref./
```

Madam,

    In confirmation of War Office telegram of the 8th April, 1943, I am directed to inform you, with regret, that a notification dated the 4th April, has been received from the Military Authorities in North Africa that your son, Captain D.A.D.J. Bethell, Royal Artillery, has been reported missing.

    No further information is available at present, but all possible enquiries are being made and any further information received by this Department will be sent to you immediately. Should you receive any communication from Captain Bethell, or should news of him reach you from any other course, will you kindly notify this Office, and at the same time forward any card or letter you may receive from him, which will be returned to you after inspection.

    In the meantime I am to ask you to be good enough to notify this Office of any change of your address.

                                         I am, Madam,
                                              Your obedient Servant,

                                              A. Williams

Mrs. D.L. Bethell,
    Bishopsdown Court,
        Tunbridge Wells.

Drew was captured on the 30th March 1943 and the first his mother knew about his fate was when she received a letter dated 10th April. "Reported missing' was often a euphemism for 'possibly killed but we can't be sure'.

The first letter is accompanied by an advice sheet that offered the unconvincing conjecture that he 'may possibly be a prisoner of war' although for a mother awaiting news of her son, the fact that 'every effort is being made to discover his fate', would have done little to assuage her anxiety.

ADVICE TO THE RELATIVE OF A MAN WHO IS MISSING

In view of the official notification that your relative is missing, you will naturally wish to hear what is being done to trace him.

The Service Departments make every endeavour to discover the fate of missing men, and draw upon all likely sources of information about them.

A man who is missing after an engagement may possibly be a prisoner of war. Continuous efforts are made to speed up the machinery whereby the names and camp addresses of prisoners of war can reach this country. The official means is by lists of names prepared by the enemy Government. These lists take some time to compile, especially if there is a long journey from the place of capture to a prisoners of war camp. Consequently " capture cards " filled in by the prisoners themselves soon after capture and sent home to their relatives are often the first news received in this country that a man is a prisoner of war. That is why you are asked in the accompanying letter to forward at once any card or letter you may receive, if it is the first news you have had.

Even if no news is received that a missing man is a prisoner of war, endeavours to trace him do not cease. Enquiries are pursued not only among those who were serving with him, but also through diplomatic channels and the International Red Cross Committee at Geneva.

The next letter comes two weeks later. It offers little comfort. Not only is he missing but now his mother knows that he is wounded. It would be hard not to assume that those wounds could be life threatening. The uncertainty causes her to put a notice in *The Times* seeking information. It seems like a long shot.

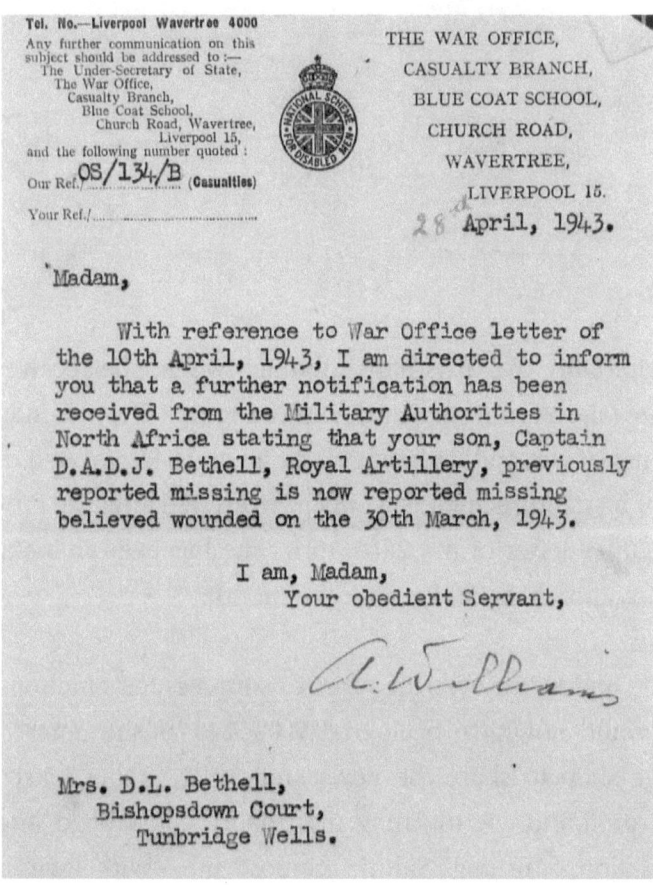

Tel. No.—Liverpool Wavertree 4000

Any further communication on this subject should be addressed to:—
The Under-Secretary of State,
The War Office,
Casualty Branch,
Blue Coat School,
Church Road, Wavertree,
Liverpool 15,
and the following number quoted:

Our Ref. OS/134/B (Casualties)

Your Ref./

THE WAR OFFICE,
CASUALTY BRANCH,
BLUE COAT SCHOOL,
CHURCH ROAD,
WAVERTREE,
LIVERPOOL 15.

28 April, 1943.

Madam,

    With reference to War Office letter of the 10th April, 1943, I am directed to inform you that a further notification has been received from the Military Authorities in North Africa stating that your son, Captain D.A.D.J. Bethell, Royal Artillery, previously reported missing is now reported missing believed wounded on the 30th March, 1943.

    I am, Madam,
    Your obedient Servant,

A. Williams

Mrs. D.L. Bethell,
Bishopsdown Court,
Tunbridge Wells.

BETHELL.—Reported missing in North Africa, D. A. D. J. BETHELL (DREW), Captain, Royal Artillery eldest son of late Hon. D. L. Bethell, of Gibraltar, brother of F/O. Tony Bethell (P.O.W.), and of Denis. Any information very gratefully received by his mother, Mrs. Bethell, 5, Bishopsdown Court, Tunbridge Wells.

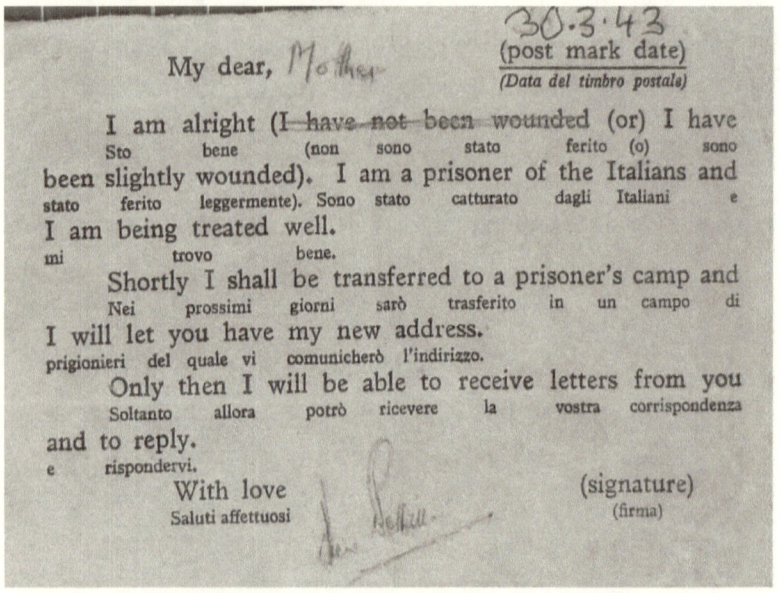

Eventually, and it is hard to gauge when, she receives the long-awaited pro forma card confirming that Drew is indeed a prisoner of war and with only slight wounds. He wrote it on the day of his capture but it can only have arrived after the previous War Office letter of the 28th April. She has been in a state of intense apprehension for almost a month.

She had learnt over the years to suppress her emotions and she would not have been overly excited as she entered the village shop to share the news and yet the relief must have been profound. A touching informality has slipped into the translation: turning 'Saluti affetuosi' into 'With love'. I am sure he would have liked to send her his love, and yet a more accurate translation would have been 'warm regards'.

Stoke Newington, London. May 2024

Dear Dad,

I wonder how much of my imagined battle for Recce Ridge would resonate with you? I was able to draw on enough first-hand testimony to be sure that the basic facts are more or less correct. You were there, the battle was fierce and you were captured. You are listed as the Forward Observation Officer for that action and as we saw you 'were reported wounded and failed to return'. But am I taking liberties with your history? That's what this book is about: trying to fill in the gaps where I so failed to ask you the right questions at a time when you might have been able to answer them. I have enjoyed the research. As I have said, there was no such thing as Google when you died in 1988. You had no idea of the satisfaction and the connection I feel when your name comes up in a first-hand account, a regimental record or a list of the missing and wounded. Each time, I want to share my excitement with you. I want to show you the references and ask about what you remember and what you felt at these critical points in your young life. But it is too late and a Google search result is a poor substitute for your voice and your remembrance.

Your obituary, written forty-five years later does mention the damage to your hearing caused by your experience on Recce Ridge.

I can find no corroboration but I do know that you were hard of hearing when I got to know you. You refused to acknowledge or discuss this. No one would have had the courage to suggest you might use hearing aids. You were too proud. In your defence it is true that hearing aids were never very discreet in your lifetime, whereas when I began to realise that I wasn't hearing well enough to chair a meeting, I had the money and the encouragement to purchase an expensive pair that hardly anyone noticed.

Your mother kept the various communications she had from the War Office in the weeks after you were captured. They tell their own story. She only received confirmation that you were alive a full month after the action at Recce Ridge. The first letter letters must have caused great distress. It doesn't say 'missing presumed dead' but surely that's what I, and I am fairly sure she must have assumed was the case. That's over a month of coming to terms with the death of your eldest son.

There were thousands of women across the country who were dealing with similar uncertainty, dreading the arrival of the next letter that would confirm their worst fears. That it was a common experience and came at a time where emotions were contained by convention and expectation, cannot have diminished the anguish. And this was a woman who had already lost her husband by his own hand. I never found her very easy to talk to and nor did you, and I am sure you never spoke about that dreadful hiatus, but I would love to know whether in all the intensity of being shipped out of North Africa and processed into a POW camp, you didn't cast your mind back to your mother, living on her own in Bishops Down Court, Tunbridge Wells.

I need to move on to the next chapter of your story. The premise of the book is that I am far too late to find answers to the questions I dearly wished I had asked whilst you were alive. But, as you would remember, in 1986 something very strange had happened that caused you to break the self-imposed omerta about your wartime experience. You had been asked to address the local Rotary Club on a subject of your choosing. And you chose to speak about your escape from that Italian POW camp and the subsequent perilous walk 450 miles along the Apennine mountains to re-join your regiment. As it happened the talk was cancelled and you were feeling disheartened when you got out the brandy at the end of dinner and then told me the story.

At one point you went to your desk and brought back a slip of paper. On it was a list of names of Italian villages. You explained that you were not able to write down anything that might incriminate the peasant farmers who had helped you on your way, but that as soon as you had made it back to safety you jotted down all the names you could remember. This was your itinerary. You had never spoken about it before and I was stunned to have a precious part of your history revealed at last. When I asked why you hadn't talked to me about it before, you replied, quite accurately I had to confess: 'Because you never asked!"

"Well" I said "I think we should make a documentary about your escape. Go and find some of the people who helped you". Those were easy words with which to beguile your father. I persuaded you to give me a copy of the ill-fated Rotary Clube talk. It was an absorbing account of your escape and I used it to garner interest and investment from friends and relatives. Somehow, much to

the astonishment of both of us, my fragile aspiration to become a television producer came to pass, and a year on from that dinner table pledge, we did set off from Heathrow to fly to Milan to start making a film about your escape. It took three weeks to shoot and it was, as I tried to persuade you, a chance to get to know each other in a way we'd never done before. You were more sanguine. But you were an enthusiastic participant and as I look at the film now I can feel the affection and the admiration that, despite the lack of an emotional catharsis, I still feel for you to this day.

I want to remind you of some of the revelatory moments from the film, which we called The Stranger at the Gate, but I also want to combine your own description as you wrote it for the good burghers of the East Grinstead Rotary Club. It is a chance to enjoy your voice: both your written voice and your actual voice from the documentary. It begins with your description of just what happened after you were captured on Recce Ridge.

Love,

Hum.

The list of locations Drew Bethell passed through on his walk down the Apennines after his escape on the 10th September 1943. He wrote it from memory once he crossed the Allied lines on October 23rd

```
10.  Woods - 2 kms from Camp.
11.  Bosca - Murat family.
12.    "
13.    "
14.  Crossed railway.
15.  Siccomonte.
16.  Parrochia. (Chicken & eggs.)
17.  Borsea - (frightened fascist.)
18.  Visigasto - priest & churishap climb.
19.  Castel Vecchio.
20.  Horrid - hill - hose! - Georgeous blonde
21.  Samoni                     10 ⎫
22.  Io hof. wan (Montese).     11 ⎬ Fragno
23.  Iola                       12 ⎭
24.  C.C.                       13  Rocca di Mezzo.
25.  Monzuno.                   14  Casoli
26.  Belvedere.                 15  Shack n. Pecasatoli
27.  S. Andrea.                 16  *Barrea.
28.  S. Maria.                  17  Castel Fiovo.
29.  Civitella.                 18.⎫ v. Cherr..
30.  Monguido. (9 gens.)        19.⎬  "   "
 1.  Altero (alone)             20. Cessano.
 2.  Valbona                    21.⎫ Frosolone.
 3.  Castelguelfo               22.⎭
 4.  Gubbio. (6 kms st.)        23. Home. P.P.C.L.I.
 5.  Morano. Giovani.               F. Lir. H.Q.
 6.  Gubbiolo - Hotel Umbera & Bishops palace.
 7.  Preci
 8.  Terracino.
 9.  Maschoria
```

MAKE SURE THAT THE ADDRESS IS WRITTEN IN LARGE BLOCK LETTERS IN THE PANEL ABOVE

This space should not be used.

CHAPTER 14

Drew's story with scenes from the film

Stranger at the Gate transmitted BBC 2.
Thursday 26th June 1988.

Drew's Account

By the time I was captured I had a grenade splinter in my shoulder and a twisted ankle. (The splinter is still there). The infantry company had 96 killed or wounded out of 111 and I was a prisoner-of-war of the Austrian Edelweiss Mountain Division. An Irish Guards Subaltern and I were the only surviving officers of six. We were escorted to Battalion Headquarters where the German C.O. questioned me in French - did we cut the ears off our prisoners? I hastened to reassure him - but there was an element of truth. The Goums - the hardy, savage, irregulars of Tunisia and Algeria were offered a bonus for every dead German they could provide. Proof was an ear. Possibly the occasional prisoner lost an ear to add to the bonus. Fortunately, the C.O. believed me.

So off to Tunis then the last ship to Naples then to Caserta, the main reception camp where we were searched thoroughly for the first time. Officers had been issued with an elementary escape kit a thin file, a front stud which concealed a small compass in the base, and maps printed in silk sewn into the lapels of the battle dress. However, the genial Italian officer who searched me had seen it all before. He took the stud scratched the enamel and tossed it in the wastepaper basket, then bent my lapel to find the file and laughed. He didn't find the map, but it hadn't much use as it was of North Africa!

A fortnight of very short commons, heat, dust and picking bed-bugs out of the stitching round our canvas cots was an introduction to PoW life. Our final destination was to be Fontanellato, PG49, on the plain of the River Po between Parma (where the ham comes from) and Piacenza. A long train journey packed into third-class carriages (we were lucky) and then a long march in the blazing heat and dust to PG 49.

The buildings had been a modern orphanage attached to a nunnery; lovely marbled floors, huge dormitories, good plumbing, gloriously cool in the heat of summer, but coolish in the winter (particularly as we used the central heating chimney to dispose of the tunnel spoil!).

I joined in that most escapist of activities - escape. We started tunneling with the disadvantage that the water table was only thirty six inches under the surface. It is a considerable test of concentration to lie on your belly in wet clay, levering away with a trowel at a face illuminated by a bare electric light bulb which occasionally shorts out and burns, filling the tin bowls with spoil, as the air-line humps and whistles beside you. The tunnel had to be reinforced the whole way, and one had to wriggle back nearly thirty yards. We were caught out by a snap search which met four officers clad in earth stained "Long Johns" on their way to the showers. Another thirty seconds and we would have got away with it. So, we lost that tunnel, and the four diggers and I got thirty days in the solitary confinement cells. The highly civilised Italian Commandant remarked "Gentlemen, I appreciate that your duty is to escape you will appreciate that mine is to prevent you: 30 days".

Stranger at the Gate

ITALY 27th September 1987.
Forty-four years after his capture on Recce Ridge, Drew returned to Italy with his son Andrew. With only a scribbled list of names, the hoped to retrace his journey and find some of the people who had helped him.

Drew and Andrew have arrived at the disused orphanage in the village of Fontanellato which, in 1943, housed the officers' POW Camp PG 39. They are sitting outside in the sunshine with a glass of beer.

Andrew: You talked about escaping. Tell me about the sort of escaping you got involved in.

Drew: Well I was recruited to this particular tunnel by some highly experienced escapers who had been in other camps and made some very dramatic escapes indeed,. I was newly arrived and I was merely slave labour. But, delighted to be asked, and delighted at the thought that one might get out. Although I must say, being at the end of a twenty-five-yard tunnel if you suffer slightly from claustrophobia, it does give one. (pause) . . it gave me the heebie-jeebies. It was very frightening and I hated it!

They have got into the disused dormitory where Drew slept.

Drew: My bed was about the middle of that wall over there.

Andrew: Just like a public-school dormitory.

Drew: No change at all, except perhaps the blankets were a bit brighter.

Andrew: And what did you do up here?

Drew: You spent a surprising amount of time in here. Reading, writing. Um. Playing cards. I learnt to play bridge here. In fact, I remember bidding seven hearts when the armistice was announced . . .and making it.

Drew's Account

On 9th September 1943 the Italians surrendered. Next day the Italian Commandant honoured his obligations and freed his prisoners: at least a hole was cut in the wire to let us stream out to the woods and then to the farms round the camp. He even provided a donkey for the officer with a broken ankle. Six hundred left just twenty made it to safety. The rest were re-captured. Two days later the Germans arrived to collect the British prisoners - found none and shot the Commandant on the spot, an honourable and gallant man.

Stranger at the Gate

Drew is looking out from the upper floor of the orphanage across the grounds where he and six hundred others had escaped from the camp

Drew: Well we all lined up and walked across the playing fields at the back of the camp and found the hole that they had cut in the wire. We went out into the maize fields and the vines beyond. We must have looked a very motley crew as we shambled in a most unmilitary fashion on our way to freedom. There was tremendous exhilaration, everybody was like schoolboys. We were out! It was wonderful stuff.

After hiding in a wide ditch for twenty-four hours, Drew teamed up with Douglas Flowerdew, older and more senior but he thought Drew looked like 'a nice-looking chap'. Together they set off to try their luck in a nearby farm house.

In the present day, Drew and Andrew visit the farm that had sheltered them. They are taken to the barn.

Farmers wife: There you are. That is where you slept all those years ago

Together they climb up a ladder into the hay loft.

Drew: I'd say the ladder we climbed up then would not have taken two of us.

Andrew: Looks pretty uncomfortable to me.

Drew: Well we couldn't have slept on these modern bales, but then the hay was laid out and very comfortable. You must remember we were free and we were fed. That's what mattered.

Drew's Account

The Italian peasants and farmers loathed and desperately feared the Germans and remarkably had respect and affection for the English. It was to be the theme of certainly my, and many others, escape. I suppose there were a dozen of us sleeping in the hay, being fed by the farmer and his large family. They could not have done it for long. The matter was resolved when rumour flashed across the Po plain that the Germans were searching for the escaped PoWs with the usual lethal penalties for those harbouring any *Tedeschi* - a word which put a shiver of horror through the simple country folk.

It was my good fortune that a Gunner Major, Douglas Flowerdew, had been planning his own escape for some time and preparing for it. He, being small and blonde, had decided to travel dressed as a woman. He had suffered the mockery of his fellows to grow his hair long. Whatever else, with his skirt, flat shoes, long blonde hair and suitable padding he earned his wolf-whistles! In his kindness, and sense of responsibility for a young fellow Gunner officer he invited me to join him. We had to go quickly but where? One alternative was Switzerland tantalisingly close, only ninety miles, but even if successful, the Swiss interned the escapee for the rest of the war, then there were rumours of landings at Leghorn (Livorno) on the west coast - about a hundred miles, but then it became clear that the only landings we could be sure of were in the South - say four hundred miles or more. We settled for the last. Our kind farmer provided a guide to the railway which we crossed, in fear of German patrols, at midnight 14th September 1943 and then walked quickly up the increasingly steepening foothills to the Apennines. Dawn found us about 10 miles away in the edge of a copse. I learnt my first Italian phrases that evening *"Io sono uffiziale Inglesi e volio trovare luogi per questa note"*. Adding *"dormire"* and *"fenile"* to sleep in the hay. We learnt to stop well before dusk, when the doors and shutters were open and the peasant family could inspect us. When the doors were bolted and shutters up, after dark, nothing would persuade them to open.

In Love And War

Stranger at the Gate

Douglas: Drew was walking better than I was. He would stop for a pause and a rest and let me catch up and then by the time I had caught up, he was eager to get on again and would stride off! One of our strongest weapons was Drew's nice smile. Drew's obviously a nice chap, then once we were in, then I would get in the corner by the fire and take my shoes off and it would hard to get rid of us at that stage.

Stuart Hall[9], another escapee remembers the experience of knocking on the door, as strangers looking for food and shelter.

Stuart: When you were on the road, there was always a moment of tension and fear that you were going to be turned away. There was always, as you knock on that door, fear, fear of rejection.

Drew and Andrew are driving on to the next location

Andrew: Why were you so trusting of the peasants?

Drew: I think their natural kindness which had been made manifest already and increasingly one realised that high up in the hills there was an innate natural goodness.

[9.] Stuart Hall wrote his own account of his time in the Apennines after his escape. Pebbles in the Skull and was interviewed for the film.

Andrew: Yes, I find that a bit too easy an answer really because they must also have been very mistrustful of people from the valley. You must have been people from the valley.

Drew: No. I think they knew...we were English!

Drew's Account

Surprisingly we did not arouse much interest - a man and woman trudging up and down the steep dusty country lanes in the blazing September sun. We were going across the grain of the country - the long spines that ran from the heights of the Apenines down to the plain. On the fifth evening we were taken by a farmer to the house of the village priest. He made us most welcome and his house-keeper lavished her best cooking on us. So, we fell into the care of the priests and, bless them, they planned, they talked, they gave us guides. to the next village, fed us and wined us splendidly. It was easier for Douglas, speaking Italian so well, he understood the endless negotiations, had learnt patience as he had been a PoW for over two years. But to an impatient young man of twenty-two, aching to be gone and away, it became too much. When the kind priests suggested waiting for three or four days for a lorry, I struck. Douglas could stay but I was going alone. He was recaptured a month later escaped again and made his way to Rome and was hidden until we liberated the City in June 1944. Two other friends were recaptured, doused in petrol by the SS and burnt to death. I add this grim note as a background to reinforce the peasant's justifiable terror. And mine!

Stranger at the Gate

> Roger Absalom: (*Historian, famous for his study of the 'strange alliance between Allied soldiers and the Italian peasants who sheltered and protected them"*)[10]
> The peasant conceived in the people he helped a way of distancing himself from the image he had always had to suffer or to live with through history, an image as an inferior, dirty smelly person who is not welcome in decent company, who is too coarse to be accepted. That is suddenly turned on its head, now he's sought after.

Drew's Account

I turned to the high hills. Dressed in a faded tartan shirt, corduroy trousers and my army boots, carrying a small sack with an army sweater, soap, razor and socks, I walked as fast as an increasingly fitter man can walk. I learnt certain rules: anyone working in a field hated the Fascists and the Germans, and whenever one came to a Y-fork always take the one that goes up (it is easier to go down from a mistake than climb again). It was a different world of tiny hill villages with no roads to them - only a donkey track. Perhaps the peasants hardly knew that there was a war on; they were busy enough wringing a living from the shallow rocky earth to worry about man's unkindness to man in the valleys and plains below. I saw incredible poverty, disease (in one village practically all the hundred souls suffered from

---

[10.] A Strange Alliance: Aspects of Escape and Survival in Italy 1943-45. La Columbaria Studi Vol 120, 1991.

trachoma) and ignorance made their kindness positively biblical.

The stranger within the gate sat down with them to their evening meal. It was usually polenta - boiled ground maize spilled over the table top and sometimes wine, but more often water. Occasionally in spite of my protests, children were made to sleep on the floor to let me have a straw filled mattress in the second family bed. And nightly the catechism started: how old was I, what was my family, my father (dead? how sad) my mother (how upset she must be) my brothers (one was a prisoner of war with the Germans, how horrible), was I really an officer (so young) was I married (my negative occasionally earned me an encouraging glance from soft dark eyes), could I drive a car, was I rich (by their standards Croesus himself). Whatever else, I learnt the rough Italian of the Apennines and Abruzzi hill villages.

Stranger at the Gate

In the car again, Andrew is probing.

Andrew: Why did you feel the need to keep walking these enormous distances and keep going and keep going?

Drew: Oh, I wanted to go back. Back to my regiment. That's who I had started the war with and I thought I'd better get back to them fairly quickly. I suppose one had an idealistic sense of duty. I just had to do it.

Drew's Account

I had been going for twenty six days when disaster struck. Scrambling down from a peak to where my "always go up" theory had led me, to a hill village in a high valley, I fell, twisting and bruising my knee. I crawled the last bit, and then the Good Samaritans of Aragno took me in - at least put me in an outhouse 200 yards above the village where they fed me, bandaged and poulticed my horribly swollen knee as well as getting the cobbler to repair my boots, all the while in constant terror of German and Fascists retribution. I lay there for the 10th, 11th and 12th October. I knew I was becoming too much of an imposition. It was becoming obvious as each day passed that my dear villagers expected someone to betray them. So, at dawn, before they could know, I left, along the sheep track on the contour of the hill over the shoulder and away to the next high slopes. It was not easy going. I did not get all that far - Rocca di Mezzo, then Cesoli and a cold hungry night in a shepherd's earth-bothy in the hill-top hamlet of Pescaseroli,

By the time I had been walking for forty days I knew I was getting close to the allied lines. There were the occasional deserted or bombed villages and increasingly I was seeing German trucks, anti-aircraft positions and I could hear the guns, and see fighter-bombers diving and soaring over roads in the valleys ahead. I became increasingly cautious, and so the pace slowed. I would stop and look out across the hills before moving across the top slopes of a valley. I had to survive on a diet of grapes. I don't recommend it.

Stranger at the Gate

A little later and Drew is musing on how memory works.

Drew: But this is difficult to explain. There is a definite impression and then long blanks when I simply don't remember. Obviously, it was just walking. Tired. Walking. Repetition. And then every now and then the whole stage is lit again and you've got this clear scene. Memory is funny that way.

Stuart Hood: What I discovered in going back is how treacherous memory is. I think one's got to be very careful about memory. Because some of the things I remember vividly are not true at all. Memory has got to be taken with a pinch of salt.

Drew and Andrew are on the Monte Marchetta, a sheltered plateau above the village of Frosolone

Drew: Yes, that's it. That's where we came

Andrew: It's an amazing place.

Drew: Well it's absolutely hidden from anywhere else. Invisible from down below

Drew's Account

I suppose Frosolone was another five terribly slow miles further on, but we arrived just before dusk to find the village on fire, the villagers panic-stricken and driving their livestock before them up the hill; men, women, children, sheep, goats, pigs, chickens with the theme song of terror - *Tedeschi, Tedeschi*. We joined them in the rush up the hill. It was too much for the old village sow. She must have had a heart attack and dropped dead as we arrived at the little plateau high on the mountain side. The villagers were starving, and so were we, in no time a bonfire was lit, invisible from the valley below, and the flames flickered on the circle of faces each concentrated on a wooden-spitted spluttering lump of sow's flesh, carved from the still warm corpse. We forgot all else in hot greasy anticipation and satisfaction. Four days of a diet of grapes followed by an extravaganza of toasted pork needs a strong stomach. Mine wasn't that strong so a horrid early morning.

But daylight revealed the long slow grassy slopes, beloved by the shepherds, which fell gently away to the south east for three miles or so to the plains of Campobasso. The hill was seething with peasantry from the villages below, with their livestock and a dozen escaped prisoners of war. Below us were the German positions.

It was a grandstand from which to watch the British attack as it started in mid-morning. We were curiously detached from the thuds and rumbles of the guns, the black-centered blossoms of smoke which merged to screen the farmhouses and woods, the "Dinky toy" tanks that advanced, fired and occasionally erupted into thick black smoke. We watched German gunners and infantry in half-tracks pulling back at mid-day. We could see the odd German infantryman moving behind a wall or hedge below, but they were not digging in, so patently only a thin patrol line. We were very lucky to find such a fluid situation. An RAF Wing Commander and I decided to cross the lines as soon as possible after dark. The RAF man and I were alone, each slightly distrustful that the other might wreck our chances having got so far by ourselves. We tossed a coin for who was to go first, agreeing that the second man would give the first five minutes start. I lost, and waited for the longest five minutes ever. It was strangely quiet, no moon, as I crept down the slopes, stopping every hundred yards to listen and search the black shadows ahead rather like a lethal form of grandmother's footsteps, expecting every moment the guttural German challenge followed by a burst of Schmeisser

It seemed to go on forever – any unfamiliar sound would have me diving sideways, eyes aching with concentration, ears tuned to the silence for the slightest click of a safety catch. And then suddenly the clip-clop of a donkey coming up the path froze me to the side of the lane until looking across I saw a mule and two men with the silhouettes of English tin helmets. I stepped down cautiously to announce that "I'm English escaped" to the two Canadian soldiers busy laying telephone lines from the reels on the mule's back. They were astonishingly calm – "Just keep on down this lane and you'll come to Battalion Headquarters". I had passed through the German and Canadian patrols and was well behind the lines! I walked on down until a sentry halted me with all the quiet confidence of a man whose battalion had pushed the Germans back three or four miles and didn't expect them back.

The Adjutant was equally relaxed, as I was ushered in - "There is not much room here anyway. The Battalion is celebrating its anniversary down the road. Why don't you join them?". A genial Canadian private walked me down to a farmhouse where practically every officer in the 2nd Battalion Princess Patricia's Canadian Light Infantry was having a ball. What a welcome: food, wine, merriment I must have told my story several times, but I suppose it was about 3 a.m. when I rolled into a sleeping bag on the floor of the Command vehicle.

They let me sleep for ten hours before they roused me, gave me a new razor, breakfast and a jeep to Bari. Quite astonishingly, the Allied powers-that-be had elected to put escaped POWs into the old Italian PoW Camp at Bari, demonstrating a reputation for careless cruelty unmatched in Italy. After my wonderful reception by the Canadians, I was not prepared to stomach it. The question uppermost in my mind was: where was my regiment? Still in Tunis was the report.

Next morning, I persuaded a jeep driver to take me out to the airfield at Bari. At the Control Tower I explained my situation to the competent, relaxed U.S. Major. Could he help? When did the next aircraft leave for Tunis? "Well, Captain" or rather "Waaal", "there is one in three minutes and another in twenty". With no ties, and no toothbrush I elected the former.

A young man dressed in a faded tartan shirt and corduroy slacks with no means of proving his identity and claiming to be a British officer didn't carry much weight in Tunis. I was escorted by an armed GI, chewing gum, to the office of the

Provost Marshal. He listened to my tale, then remarked that it was so improbable that it must be true - a perceptive, kind man. So almost seven months to the day, I rejoined my regiment; a remarkable institution bound by discipline, loyalty, history, pride in efficiency, shared experience and recently shared sorrow.

I had come home.

Stranger at the Gate

Final thoughts spoken over the credits.

Drew: It was fascinating to go back to Italy again after forty-three years. And the people recognised me unbidden which is quite an achievement. Bald, old and deaf, they still recognised me. I was very flattered. And touched. But the distance! It was a very long way to walk. When I look at it *now, I wonder whether I can walk across a room unaided.*

Drew rejoined his regiment and went on to fight in Italy until the liberation was complete.

In Love And War

Drew Bethell died suddenly on February 6th 1988, six weeks after this film was completed.

Stoke Newington, London, June 2024

Dear Dad,

I have been lucky enough to have spent the last few weeks in your company as I transcribed your words from that film. I am lucky that I can do that. I hear your voice, watch your mannerisms and it reminds me of both your strengths and your vulnerabilities. You were a willing participant in telling your own story. And yet you did not give much away. As you reminded me during that scene in the pizza restaurant:" One wasn't encouraged to speak about oneself". And yet so much of your charm and your enthusiasm comes across. And then I was able to marvel at your lucid prose and fine story-telling in that first telling of the story prepared for the Rotary Club. They don't know what they missed.

I have not transcribed the scenes where you are engaging with the many elderly Italians who really did seem to remember you. Like you, they would have been in their twenties in 1943 and they were so pleased to see you and be reminded of that time when, as Roger Absolem says, "they were sought after" rather than looked down upon. Your Italian was rudimentary and grammatically incorrect and like me you didn't understand most of what was being said back to you and yet you communicated through your exuberant body language and the odd phrase. You knew that communication in a foreign language was so much more than using the correct words. The confidence in connecting through energy, enthusiasm and charm was, I like to think, a quality you passed onto me. And although the recurring gag whereby you always introduced me as "Mi piccolo filio" did wear a bit thin, it always warmed the first encounter. I, of course, was over two metres tall, so much hilarity ensued.

The end of the film is cathartic and I have to confess to you that when that last frame comes up with the reference to your death I did weep for you. You died over thirty years ago and, as I have said, we Bethell men do not do crying, especially not in front of each other. Your death was a shock, but as with the death of my brother, my emotional demands were focused on my mother's grief. Not much room for my own. So, if I am honest there is still much grief unfelt. I suppose this book is part of that process and seeing that picture of me and you with my arm reaching to hold you, touched the wellspring of my long-buried heartache.

I was pleased that we had been able to show you an edited version of the film and you approved. You wanted us to correct the number of Irish Guardsmen who were killed on Recce Ridge which we had under-recorded. (And yet you never spoke to me about what happened there which is why I had to re-construct it). You didn't say much else about the film. I suspect we would have liked you to be a bit more effusive, but that was not your way. I hope that somewhere you had feelings of pride in your own exploits and in the achievement of your son in getting it turned into a film. You didn't live long enough to see it broadcast on BBC 2 and I sometimes conjecture how you would have dealt with the public exposure. Perhaps it was better that you weren't around.

The ending of the film also includes the sentence "Drew Bethell rejoined his regiment and went on to fight in Italy until the liberation was completed". That was in October 1943 and the Italian campaign finally ended in February 1945. That's sixteen months of your war about which, once again, I know nothing. Your silence is echoed in the absence of coverage in the received history of the Second World War. The Italian campaign was just as grueling as the arduous slog to reach Berlin after the triumphs of D Day, and yet it is barely referred to in the documentary and fictional accounts of the war. Most of my generation will have heard of the battle for the fortified monastery of Monte Cassino, but little else. It is a forgotten campaign.

Yet I am lucky because I have your regimental records for that whole period, I can trace your progress and travel with you and the 19th Field Regiment Royal Artillery. What I do know is that after you crossed the lines in October 1943 and returned to your regiment in Tunis you were given some leave back home. You might even have spent Christmas with your mother. Then in March 1944 you rejoined your regiment in Italy. What I didn't know, and you didn't tell me, was that you arrived back when 96/97 Battery was dug in two miles inland from the landing beaches of Anzio. This was the ill-fated Anzio Beach Head where thirty thousand allied troops had been penned in by the Germans for two months. It meant that for you and the 19th Field Regiment there was still another three months of what felt like a re-run of the Somme. A state of terrible stasis stuck in appalling conditions under almost constant artillery bombardment. I knew virtually nothing about

Anzio, but I do now. I feel I have been there and although the British Commander, General Sir Harold Alexander, was adamant that it was not another Dunkirk, you must have felt like you were going back in time.

With love,

Hum.

CHAPTER 15

The Anzio Beach Head

Pagdilione Woods, Anzio. March 17th 1944

I am on the edge of another crowded war-torn beach, but unlike Dunkirk this is a short beach and it is ours. Behind me is what is left of the town of Anzio (some say the birthplace of both Nero and Caligula). A few facades remain standing from what would have been a charming Italian sea front but most of the buildings have been reduced to rubble that spills out onto street. In front of me LST 360 is bashing its way up the beach towards me as I sit on a what remains of a bench outside what was once a café.

The LST (Landing Ship Tanks) is not a pretty ship, but it is efficient at carrying large numbers of troops and their heavy armoured equipment close into a landing site and in this case right onto the seafront. They are made and owned by the Americans but have been lent to us under the Lend Lease Act that gave the British Army much needed access to military hardware from 1941 to 1944. At its front LST 360 has two huge doors which, once it had ground to a stop, open wide to port and starboard to reveal a ramp which crashes down onto the flattened sand and gravel laid a month ago to facilitate the unloading of a steady stream of supplies required to support a stranded army.

First out of the hold come replacement M4 Sherman tanks of the American Armoured Division. They rumble and clank their way down the ramp and once on dry land they start to churn up the compressed gravel as the GI sitting in the turret gives the order to turn right and one track holds back as the other track drives the beast round. Then comes another and another. The LST can carry eighteen Sherman tanks, but on this day just seven emerge onto the seafront. They are followed by fifteen ten-ton lorries. I know that these are full of artillery rounds mostly 25 lb shells that will be fired by the British Royal Artillery regiments of which the 19th Field is just one of ten. They have been shelling the enemy almost constantly for the last six weeks with often as many as one hundred rounds per day. There is an urgent need for more ammunitions as the engagement is far from over.

The LST has also brought in a hundred and sixty troops as replacements for the several thousand men who have been either killed or wounded defending the Anzio Beach Head. I have an interest in just one of those men on board and I think I can see him amongst the figures watching the unloading from the prow of the ship. I can't be sure it is my father but I do know he will be on this ship because today is the day he is re-joining his regiment after his successful escape from PG49 some five months ago. It took more than a month after he crossed the allied lines at Frosolone before arrangements were made to ship him back to the UK for some restorative leave and top-up training. Now he is back, As I try to identify his British helmet amongst the majority of Americans. I know he has a birds-eye view of the town and the fields beyond where the signs of war may be hard to discern. It is flat agricultural land, stretching away towards a range of hills. He has no idea of the significance of those hills. They are the Alban Hills now fortified by the Germans to provide immense artillery fire power to rain down on the beach head. I am wondering how much he knows of what is in store and what has happened here in the last two months.

I have also spotted an officer with the Royal Artillery flashes on his grubby tunic. He too is looking up at the men on the prow. I wonder if he can identify my father because I know they are brother officers in 19th Field Regiment. In fact, it is Temporary Captain David Blake who joined the regiment in September 1941. He will have missed Dunkirk but will have served with my father until the day of his capture on Recce Ridge in 1943, almost exactly a year ago. But he is a rare breed in the 19th. What my father does not know, but Captain Blake is acutely aware of, is that in the last six weeks the regiment has lost 14 officers: four killed and ten wounded badly enough to be taken off the beach head. Of thirty-six officers currently on roll, eighteen will be unknown to my father most having joined after the worst of the fighting in February.

But now I see him emerge onto the ramp of LTS 360, his clean khaki battle dress standing out from the grey uniforms of the American GIs who are swarming down the ramp with him.

I do notice that he now has two pips on his shoulder. He was a Temporary Captain when captured, but he seems to have been dropped back to the lowlier rank of Lieutenant. He cannot see me because I am, once again, an ethereal time traveller, but he spots David and I am close enough to see his broad open smile that so endeared him to the Italian contadini. They shake hands and David grabs my father's kitbag and they begin to walk north along the front and then into the edge of Podglione Wood. I cannot hear what they are saying but it is clear that once they get past the pleasantries, the talk becomes serious. My father will have asked: "So what's been happening?"

"We had an easy landing and got the guns into the wood, the one ahead of us. Initially we reckoned we'd caught the Germans by surprise and they were too busy defending the Gustav Line and Monte Cassino. In fact, that was the case[11]. But the Germans did not hang around and almost immediately they were pouring in reinforcements. I remember looking across at the Alban Hills on the second night and it seemed alive with headlights criss-crossing the side of the mountain. Those were the reinforcements that were going to make our lives hell.[12]

---

11. From the theatre commander, Field Marshal Albert Kesselring, on down, no one had seen this coming. Just days earlier, Admiral Wilhelm Canaris, chief of German military intelligence (Abwehr), had visited Kesselring's headquarters in Frascati and reported that he didn't see "the slightest sign of an imminent landing in the near future." Ship traffic in Naples harbor was normal. "You can sleep easy tonight," Canaris told the boss.
12. Field Marshal Albert Kesselring was in overall command of German forces in Italy and a contingency plan for such a landing was already in place. He redeployed the Fourteenth Army from its bases near Rome, and summoned reinforcements from northern Italy, France and Germany. He requested as many troops as could be spared from the Tenth Army defending the Gustav Line. By 25 January elements of five divisions - 40,000 German troops - under the command of General Eberhard von Mackensen had surrounded the Allied Beach Head.

"Look up there, do you see the hills? Well it's the perfect observation position They can see our every move to direct their guns which they had dug in up there and later when more armament arrived in the valley a few miles from our lines. It all happened within the first few days of our` arrival and they have been shelling us relentlessly ever since. We are sitting ducks. We cannot retreat into the sea, so all we can do is dig in. The Germans locate us during night firing. The flash of each gun gives us away. Then there are the mortars. They can creep up the wadis[13] and set up their mortars and they do as much damage as the big guns from further back. It has been grim, we've lost a lot of men. Over twenty killed and many more wounded. They leave the line and are taken back to Naples for medical treatment. Not many get back to us. You won't have heard that we lost the C.O. Colonel Hamilton. He was killed just two weeks ago from a direct hit on his dugout. Did you know Richard Grieg? He took over, and seems to be doing well, bit of a stickler which is right and proper, it's just that we've all had a hell of a pasting and it's not surprising that the OR's (Other Ranks) are getting a bit slack. We are shooting up to a hundred rounds per day and night. We've never done that rate of fire before and it is gruelling."

I am following Acting Captain Blake and Lieutenant Bethell as they walk through the woods. They are having to walk around craters filled with filthy water, past burnt out lorries and then skirt round the encampments where each unit has established a Command Post. Camouflaged netting strung

[13.] The area around Anzio was marshy with wide drainage ditches. The British troops fresh from fighting in Africa where the dry sandy gullies were called wadis, transplanted the term to describe the wet muddy ditches where they were to do much of their fighting.

up over radio aerials, tents dug into the ground and officers bent over trestle tables. The uniforms are barely recognisable, covered in mud and if those officers do look up I am struck by the gaunt emptiness of men deprived of any consistent sleep by the impact of the persistent shelling of their positions. But my father is still striding along. He has plenty of energy. His batteries are re-charged. His uniform is presentable and as they arrive at the regimental HQ of 19th Field Regiment he straightens up and pulls his shoulders back. He is about to meet his new commanding officer, the recently appointed Colonel Grieg. They salute and Blake makes the introductions:

"Sir, I don't think you know Drew Bethell. He was captured at Recce Ridge in Tunisia last year."

"Excellent. Good to have you back. I gather you escaped and walked back to our lines. That's quite a walk. How long did it take you?"

"Six weeks sir. We made pretty good time."

"Well we're very pleased to have you back. As you know it has been a tough show and it doesn't look as if it is getting any easier. David, do we know where Drew will be lodging?"

"Sergeant Major told me to give him Brian Paterson's digs. He was wounded last week."

"Well make sure it's properly protected. They tell me that you need to cover the roof in ammo boxes filled with earth.

1944

Apparently, it does a pretty good job of keeping out the worst. Of course, it can't stand a direct hit as we now know! Drew, get yourself settled and then report to your Battery Commander. You're with 96/97 aren't you? We're going to need you on FOP duties (Foreword Observation Posts). We've lost a couple of OP officers in the last few weeks."

"Yes, sir. Thank you, sir. I'll do my best".

One more salute and David Blake leads my father off into the woods. Like me, he understands the significance of the OP assignment.

"You were FOO[14] at Recce Ridge weren't you? This is a bit different but still can be dicey. They are fixed OP points, and they are pretty well dug in, but the enemy are so damned close that the mortar fire can be pretty bloody".

I can see my father has lost a little of his zest for action. He doesn't need reminding that as an FOO, however well dug in, you are still exposed and vulnerable. That's the point. You have to be way out in front of your guns to direct their fire.

David Blake has stopped and at first it is hard to see where my father will sleep. The ammunition boxes are there and I can see them resting on a wooden roof to what looks like a trench. Barely the size of a coffin. There's a camp bed and an orange box with a half-burnt candle. The bedding is a pretty unsavoury looking blanket. This will be home for my father

14. FOO: Forward Observation Officer

for the next two months. I remember him talking about feeling claustrophobic in the tunnel at Fontanellato and wonder whether it will kick in again should he be woken, suddenly, by an enemy bombardment and rise up from his bed to hit his head on the roof. But at least I am reassured that my father will be safe as long as he avoids the fate of his erstwhile and ill-fated Lieutenant Colonel Hamilton killed when his dugout suffered a direct hit.

Then as evening approaches, my father is in with his Battery Commander hearing about his first OP assignment. I can see him starting to shiver because it is the middle of March and this has been an unseasonal period of cold weather and there is no sign of spring. I remember that insubstantial army blanket back in my father's dugout and I know he is going to be cold tonight. If the guns don't wake him then the cold surely will.

At the Anzio Beach Head, my father's regiment were located in the Eastern Sector in support of three infantry brigades. They were fighting on the ground in front of the guns, attacking enemy positions and trying to establish control of the hinterland. This was a terrifying war zone where the enemy could be anywhere hidden in the wadis. It was a war of attrition not unlike the battles of the First World War. The diary of an infantry soldier described the battle field in just those terms:

> So back we go to WW1. Oozing thick mud. Tank hulks. The cold, God the cold. Graves marked by a

*helmet gashed with shrapnel. Strands of barbed wire.
Trees like broken fish bones.*

The gun positions were regularly bombed at night. In amongst the high explosive shells from the enemy's big guns, aircraft would drop anti-personnel bombs. These were called 'butterfly bombs' and consisted of a container holding about a hundred small grenade type objects. The container exploded about two hundred feet above the ground and showered its contents over the area, with the grenades fragmenting on impact and spraying shrapnel. If one of these caught any troops out in the open then the effect was devastating. Luckily the sound of the aircraft gave due warning and most men would have found cover before the grenades hit the ground.

It is morning on the Anzio Beach Head. It is a grey day made worse by the residual smoke from the smoke pots that have been lit to provide a thick pall across the battle field to obscure the Allies' positions from the Germans. It is a foul smelling, black and greasy coating clothing skin and nostrils with a thin mask of carbonised oil that stifles breathing and made everyone feel dirty. I am watching my father's dugout for signs of life. He needs to be up soon as I know that this will be the start of his three-day stint as one of the regiment's OPs. I see the make-shift curtain across the doorway stir as he wriggles out. It doesn't look as if he slept much. His fellow soldiers will have got used to the sounds of enemy shells landing and ours being fired. But he is new here and he will have been woken by each thunderous detonation. And then there was the cold! I can see it in his face and in the way he eventually stands up and massages feeling back into his stiffened joints. I am pleased to say that he has put in his false teeth and despite the washed-out pallor, he still has the face of a twenty-three-year-old and he has managed to run a comb through his slicked back hair that I recognised on the beach at Dunkirk. It was the fashion back then and he wore his hair that way for the rest of his life.

In fact, I know what that first night was like because the Regimental Diary tells me that it was a calamitous one:

17th March : 96/97 Bty areas harassed by 88-mm gun – 2 ORs killed by direct hit on dugout.

96/97 Battery is my father's. He will have known those nameless Other Ranks. Had those shells killed or wounded an officer his name would be recorded in the diary, but such is the hierarchical tradition of the army, Other Ranks are not granted that privilege. They remain anonymous.

My father is not yet aware of the death of those men and he is purposeful, there is a spring in his step. He gets to the generator where he meets up with his two signallers who are charging up the batteries they will need to power the two radio sets that they will take out to the OP. My father greets the signallers with a cheerfulness that is not reciprocated. They know that two of their mates were killed overnight and they are in no mood to give a cheery response to the fresh-faced officer they barely know. They too are replacements. The stable camaraderie of a regular army regiment has been badly strained by the casualties sustained at Anzio.

They have quite a journey ahead of them. First, they will get a lift to within a mile or so of the wadi that leads to their OP. It's out to the left of them in front of the 24th Guards Brigade HQ. They will be supporting those regiments as they try to re-take the battered small town of Aprila which has been re-named The Factory because of the wrecked industrial buildings on its outskirts. It has been the scene of persistent ferocious fighting, often hand to hand, for the last two months. Despite early success, the Germans have re-taken the area and the two Guards battalions are out in the wadis preparing yet another assault to try to take it back. They will need accurate artillery support. My father is on his way to make sure they get it.

They have been dropped off at the mouth of a wadi that leads out into the battle field. They will have to carry the signalling gear: two radio sets, a drum of cable and spare acid batteries as well as rations and a four gallon can of water, they will be in the OP for three days. It is a hard slog made worse by the mud that clags onto their boots. It is cloying nasty stuff that is hard to stand up in. There are curses as they stumble along under their heavy loads. It is called the 'Oh God Wadi', and as I follow my father and his signallers I can see why.

Now they are approaching the OP which is a look-out post dug into a ridge with a good view over the ravaged farmland and the network of wadis that lead up to The Factory. They must crawl the last few yards to keep out of sight of the enemy who are watching, just as my father will be watching them. They are in the mud that cakes their battle dress. It is rank and will stink. They have run out the telephone cable that leads back to the regimental HQ. It is vulnerable and they are hoping that it does not get hit by mortar fire as that will involve a dangerous repair job.

The OP itself is pretty well protected and I feel relieved as my father hunkers down behind a protective screen with an unobtrusive slit that allows him a good view of the area. His first task is to identify where the German batteries are located and call up the first barrage of the day. His line to the Guards HQ meant he knows when and where they will attack. He has to be sure that his targets are well ahead of those troops. There can be no risk that a misplaced shell kills one of his own.

He is calling out distances and inclinations. With his binoculars he is tracking each barrage and calling back adjustments. He is self-assured in this role. He knows exactly what is required of him and he delivers precisely the right amount of detailed information in the clipped jargon that he has mastered since his training at the OCTU, just three and a half years ago. They are the same instructions he delivered from his more precarious OP on Recce Ridge and although seemingly less dangerous, my father will already have established that three different FOOs have been wounded in the last six weeks. Those mortars could still do him some damage, if not kill him.

Before long, it is time to brew up. One signaller has been assigned to make the tea and I am glad my father will have something warm inside him. He puts the steaming mug onto the makeshift shelf by the side of his viewing slit and raises his binoculars. At that moment a mortar shell lands on the face of the embankment, the explosion is amplified in the cramped space and I am deafened as a hail of soil and stones batters the front of the observation slit. My father is distracted more by the fact that his mug has fallen off the shelf than by the fact that a few yards closer and they could have been done for.

The homely reassurance of his mug of tea belies the horrors of the mutilated landscape that stretches away from him. And then there is the smell. As a newcomer to Anzio he will still be acutely conscious of the background smell, especially out here on the battlefield where so many have died in the previous weeks. Mixed in with the oily odour of the smoke machines is the putrefying smell of death. Although every effort has been made to remove the dead bodies left by the constant fighting, the close proximity to the enemy means it is often too dangerous and the bodies are left to rot. Looking through my father's observation slit I can see several bloated bodies lying in the mud. One is spread-eagled and trapped in one of the ubiquitous coils of barbed wire. It appals me and I can only speculate as to how it makes my father feel. This is the first day and he will be coming to grips with the harsh reality of the war that is being played out in the wadis and embankments that mark the outer edges of the beach head.

As with so much warfare, the role of an artillery forward observer is made up of brief burst of intense and often frightening activity, followed by long stretches of boredom. I notice my father has extracted a somewhat battered page of newsprint from his inside pocket. It is the Times crossword and he is tussling with a cryptic clue. I recognize that purposeful concentration: the furrowed brow and the tip of the tongue protruding. He would 'have a stab' at the Times crossword whenever there was a quiet moment until the day he died. He could complete the puzzle given the time and space, but he has to stick at it which is why it is a perfect way to pass the time as the men of the Scots Guards manoeuvre up the wadis to attack the tenacious German defences around The Factory.

Mortars are certainly alarming, but the real danger could just as easily come from the sky. The Germans have light planes that are capable of dropping anti-personnel bombs and grenades. So, it is no wonder that when the two signallers hear the drone of a low flying aircraft, they drop to the floor of the OP. My father, despite his almost fatal encounter with a Stuka on the beaches of Dunkirk, is slower to move. The truth is his hearing has never fully recovered from the close encounter with the hand grenade prior to his capture on Recce Ridge. At last, he hears the aircraft but before he has a chance to copy his savvier signallers, the sound of the plane starts to fade. There will be no bombs today. But as he returns to the observation slit my father sees the flutter of paper. He is confused, but his signallers are not.

"Bloody hell. Not again!"

"What's going on?"

"It's the leaflets, sir. They drop 'em on us. Meant to make us down hearted, but they're a bit of a laugh. Handy for wiping your arse. Sir!"

"Thank you, Lance Bombardier. Most instructive."

"I'll pop out and get one for you, sir"

Before my father can object, he is out of the shelter and returns with a poorly printed leaflet. On the front is a line drawing of an American GI getting into bed with a scantily clad woman with the caption: 'This is what is happening to your wives back home'.

I know that my father isn't married and I'm pretty certain he doesn't even have a girlfriend, so as a piece of propaganda it is even less likely to work with him. Whether or not he wiped his arse with it, I shall never know because I have left the OP, and of course, I was never really there.

It took the British 1st Division another two months before there was any attempt to break out of the Anzio Beach Head. Two months of sporadic engagement with no significant movement on either side. It was stalemate but with constant artillery fire going both ways and deadly low-key action as infantry patrols hunted in the wadis in what were usually inconsequential incursions into enemy territory. For the gunners of the 19th Field

Regiment it was nightly firing on VICTOR targets. These were locations that were chosen by Divisional HQ and at a given time every gun of the three artillery regiments in the same sector would fire simultaneously on the same bearing and distance. It was concentrated fire power and must have damaged the morale of those on the receiving end.

The break out eventually came at the end of May. Operation BUFFALO was a coordinated plan to attack the German positions with all three Divisions: two Americans and one British. The continual bombardment had taken its toll of the German positions and the resistance was largely limited although it still took them several days to take back The Factory.

A Major D.J.F. Grant, a Royal Artillery staff officer, wrote about the experience of finally leaving the entrenched positions and moving forward into enemy territory:

> *The divisional artillery extricated itself with difficulty from its excavations and began moving forward. To leave the Beach Head area where we had so long been penned in and harassed by shelling was a strange and exhilarating experience, and we could now all see the evidence of the destructive power of our artillery. The whole landscape was pitted with shell marks, ammunition blown up, dugouts fallen in. Not a tree bore any foliage, not a house was left standing. Roads and tracks were almost impassable for shell holes. Dead men and horses lay unburied where they had fallen. Compared with conditions within our side*

of the Beach Head which we had thought pretty bad, this was complete desolation.

I can imagine my father's exhilaration because it would be much the same as he described on being released from the POW camp at Fontanellato

The regimental diary for that period is succinct but it is clear that 1st Division made good progress towards Rome:

- *On the night of 25/26 May. 1st Division advanced on the ANZIO-ROME ROAD and entered the FACTORY.*

- *Enemy opposition was not strong. Many PoWs taken. Once on our objectives, a few enemy S.P.s (self-propelled guns) and tanks caused some trouble, but no large-scale counter attack was made by the enemy.*

- *Little opposition was met as the enemy had withdrawn the bulk of his forces, but the advance was slow in order to reduce casualties and fatigue.*

- *During the night of 3/4th June the enemy had withdrawn the bulk of his forces and the regiment crossed the TIBER on the 5th June.*

- *5th June: No rounds fired by any gun during the previous 24 hours. This being the first time the*

> *regiment had been silent for such a period since landing at ANZIO.*

The contrast between the stasis of the Anzio Beach Head and the momentum that takes them across the Tiber must have been invigorating. And they were to be rewarded for their privations.

- *GENERAL NOTES for the Month of July 1944: The month was spent on leave and training. Regimental and Battery firing practice and exercises were carried out on the Maccarese Range.*

- *22nd July: 1st Infantry Brigade Exercise NEMESIS to practice quick follow up of a retreating enemy.*

- *30th July: Visit of His Majesty the King.*

Maccarese is some twenty kilometres to the west of Rome. It sounds like a very relaxed month and I can only conjecture how my father spent his time in or near Rome. I wonder if he did a tour of the sights. Despite having been in the Army Class at school he had a decent knowledge of the classics. Would he have visited the Colosseum, then driven past the Athenaeum on his way to the Trevi fountain and the Pantheon? I want to imagine him staring up at the hole in the roof of the Pantheon and watching the dust of war dance in the sun beam as it tracks across the floor tiles made from Giallo Sense marble in patterns that date back two thousand years. I would love that to be true, although he never mentioned it to me.

What I do know is that even though they will have practised "quick follow up of a retreating enemy" there was going to be nothing quick about the next nine months of the campaign to push the Germans up and out of Italy. Theirs was a dogged retreat with every kilometre defended to the last possible moment, over some of the most challenging landscape the men of 19th Field Regiment were ever going to encounter. I hope my father enjoyed his month of training and leave in Rome reassured by the misapprehension that the battle for Italy was almost over.

Stoke Newington, London July 2024

Dear Dad,

I have had to use a lot of imagination to create your time at the Anzio Beach Head. However, much of it ought to ring true as I spent a good deal of time on research: reading first-hand accounts of what it was like, some from young artillery officers like yourself. I was amazed to discover that your regiment had played a part in the Anzio landing and the subsequent harrowing defence of that wedge of occupied Italy. Anzio was an under-recorded and yet infamous battleground where the allied forces were held up in a state of deadly stasis for over four months. Initially I was enthusiastic in creating your experience of the landing and the horrific first few weeks when the Germans hounded the allied troops with devastating fire power. That was a time of intense drama and a fearsome number of deaths and casualties. I had you in the middle of all that and was doing my best to put myself in your shoes as the German onslaught reached its crescendo in February.

Then, when I was finally able to check the list of officers on duty with 19th Field at Anzio, I learnt to my surprise and, yes, I have to confess, disappointment, that Lieutenant D A D J Bethell, re-joined the regiment on March 17th 1944 some seven weeks after the landing. Things had quietened down by then. You had avoided the worst, and all my careful re-creation had gone to waste. I could of course have faked it and had you in on the landing and the first six terrible weeks. Nobody would know. Anyone likely to challenge the dates is long gone, and I could have made up a far more exciting narrative for you. And since a lot of this is imaginary anyway, what would be the harm? But it is important to me that I stick to the parameters laid down by actual documentary evidence. I am not writing a fantasy account of your war. I am trying to answer the questions that I never got to ask. If I fake the dates and make up the locations, then I will have lost my sometimes tenuous connection to your actual story. My account of Recce Ridge is accurate in terms of dates and timings and reports of what happened, I have just placed you into an existing narrative. So, since the records show that you did not arrive at the Anzio Beach Head until March 17th, then that is when I needed to begin my description of your time there.

As for the description of what it was like in the observation post, I am taking some liberties because the regimental records do not name the FOO's unless they were either killed or wounded, and yet I dearly hope that if you were to read it, you would recognise the scene. There is no doubt that as a Lieutenant you would have been on OP duty. That was your role in 96/97 Battery. I am also reassured because just after I finished writing that, I had another stroke of luck and discovered the papers of your commanding officer Lieutenant Colonel Grieg in the Imperial War Museum. He has written his own account of the regiment's time on the beach head. Colonel Grieg writes about what it was like to be an FOO and in particular about the experience of the OP dug into the bank near the notorious Flyover outside The Factory. Based on his description,

I think both he and you would recognise my re-creation.

Seeing your name on the list of officers with their UK addresses that Colonel Grieg seemed to have kept and updated throughout the war, each iteration with a hand decorated font page, gave me an unexpected jolt of filial connection. Blessed as you and I have been with a name that appears early in any alphabetical list, your name was on the first page, just before Captain R. Blunt who was killed a few weeks before you arrived. You are there with your mother's address, ready just in case Colonel Grieg needed to write with the details of your demise. And yet, I am pleased to report that between now and the end of the war, he had no cause to write to Mrs D L. Bethell, 5 Bishopsdown Court, Tonbridge Wells, Kent. My very existence depended on that.

So now we move on to the next stage of your war. I have got you to Rome where I do hope you enjoyed yourself. The regimental records make it clear that after the relentless bombardments of the Anzio beach head and the push to cross the River Tiber all the men of the 1st Division deserved a break. Once the city had been deemed safe, I know troops were driven in to enjoy the sights and the pleasures of the night clubs where they were royally ripped off by the Italian hostesses who charged exorbitant fees for a mere dance. God knows what more intimacy would have cost you, had you been interested.

Apparently, there was a Divisional bathing beach at the Ostia Lido that had been a popular resort of the pre-war Romans. The Germans had covered it in barbed wire and mines but your engineers cleared it and set up a canteen to provide a bathing beach for the troops. The trouble was none of you had bathing suits, so as it was men only, all went naked. I am trying to imagine that scene of men and officers all frolicking in the sea and then you emerging relaxed in your nakedness. I wonder if the battering your eardrums had taken at Recce Ridge meant you could not put your head under water. That was certainly the case when in my childhood we swam, you would not participate in the fun, taking great care not to get water in your ears as with next to no ear drums it would have caused almost immediate infection. Of course, you had been a very strong swimmer at school so perhaps you swum out to deeper calmer waters with your head held high.

Then, in the first week of August, the Division went back into action. You were moved up to the outskirts of Florence to take part in the next offensive. The Germans were retreating and I imagine you thought the next bit was going to be easier. But as we will see from General Kesselring's instructions, they were not going to go quietly. They were withdrawing to the mountains. The same Apennines that you had walked down nine months earlier. You knew how damned steep and unforgiving that landscape would be. And to make matters worse, winter was approaching. In one letter to my mother, written nine months later, you make it clear that you 'so loathed' this part of your war. As I dug into the records, I could see why.

I have tracked the 19th Field regiment from Florence to Monte Grande. It is a torturous journey. From village to village, mountain to mountain you backed up the infantry battalions who were trying to break down stubborn German defences dug into the high ground. Grezzano, Pratolino and then Borgo San Lorenzo,

Monte Senario, Monte Toncane and Monte Calderaro. I wonder if those names would ring any bells. Would they conjure up visual reminders of those days and nights? I am not going to try and track your every step. That would be tedious. But I am interested in those visual memories. Those scenes that, had we sat down to talk about this part of your war and even found a way to visit the locations, as we did the villages you passed through on your walk, you might have described what it was like, what you saw and even, what it felt like. It will be like another film and I will be the film maker. Only this time you won't be able to play your part nor will you be able to judge whether I have conjured up scenes that you might recognise. Let's see how I get on.

Love

Hum

German Battle Orders for troops defending Italy 1944

Within the limits of the delaying action, every opportunity is to be taken of destroying enemy forces that have pushed ahead incautiously, and of inflicting heavy losses through action of combined arms. Withdrawal to the individual defence lines and the delaying action between them are dependent on the enemy advance. Withdrawal movements must only take place as a result of overwhelming enemy pressure or of heavy losses caused by intense artillery fire. The practice is to be followed of intensifying our own artillery fire shortly before withdrawal, and posting rear-guards well supplied with ammunition to screen the withdrawal movement.

Generalfeldmarschal Kesserling
August 1944

CHAPTER 16

Breaking the Gothic Line

Florence to Monte Grande.
August 1944 to January 1945

Scene 1: On The Road

It is very early on the morning of 4th August 1944. There is movement in the air: the regiment is ready to travel. The sun has yet to rise and the mist still hangs over the line of ten-ton tractors with twenty-five pounder guns attached at the rear. I can see men standing round in anticipation. The smoke from their cigarettes caught in the headlights of the beetle backed Morris C8 gun tractors. Squat solid work horses that have an ammunition trailer attached to the back and a gun attached to the trailer. Twenty-four tractors towing twenty-four guns. There were other supply vehicles and the convoy stretches back into the dark, their headlights creating menacing shadows from the pine trees that surround them.

It has been peaceful resting up in the pine forests south west of Rome. But it couldn't last and over the last few days they have been waiting for the order to move. Yesterday I watched my father as he and the other officers were briefed on the next stage of the campaign. The Germans had withdrawn and were now reinforcing the Gothic Line that stretched from Florence along the line of the Arno in the west, across the Apennines to Rimini in the East. 1st Division was moving up to the area south of the Arno between the city and Pontesieve a few miles to the east to relieve 4th Division. The task was to take part in the next big advance pushing the Germans out of the city and back to the mountains. They had a long drive ahead of them.

At six am, the order was passed down the line and I hear the throaty splutter as the tractor engines were fired up. The men put out their cigarettes and climb aboard: six to a tractor in a cabin behind the driver. The sun is lighting the topmost branches of the pines as the brakes are released with a sigh. I am sitting with my father in the passenger seat of the second tractor of the eight guns that make up 96/97 Battery. He has a map on his lap and he is cheerful. It has been good to spend time away from the battle especially after the ordeal of Anzio, but he is pleased to be on the move. He is bantering with the driver who has just clashed the gears, causing my father to boast of his ability to 'double de-clutch' a procedure required to get the best out of the sporty second-hand Lagonda he had managed to buy when on leave after his escape.

If I were making a film today, I would use a drone to fly high above the convoy as it snaked through the outskirts of Rome and into the lush farmland on their way north. I can imagine the music swelling as the drone soars back along the mile-long column of artillery. In transit. It would lift the spirits. The drone would zoom in to show a close up of a cheerful driver waving happily. But then the music would come to an abrupt conclusion: the column has stopped. After just half an hour, one of the Morris C8 Gun Tractors has broken down. The signal to halt is passed back and the whole convoy grinds to a stop. There has been a transmission failure in the tractor in front of my father's. He does not take it well and he reminds me of his response to being stuck in a traffic jam on the way to the seaside. Impatient and tetchy. It is the frustration that comes when a man who is used to moving onward, must accept that there are greater forces at work. Five members from the regiments Light Aid Detachment (the team of engineers attached to each regiment) have driven up in a jeep and unload their tools. My father cannot stay in his seat. He jumps down to make inquiries: I am uncertain quite how that will help.

"What's the problem Sergeant?"

"Transmission, Sir. I think we can fix it, but it means we have to get it jacked up. Take a while, Sir"

"Well, get cracking. We've got a long way to go."

"I know that sir."

The LAD do indeed get cracking and half an hour later the tractor is back on the road and the convoy can move again. However, I know that it will be a frustrating day for the regiment and my father in particular. I have read the regimental War Diary:

> *The journey caused approximately 20 mechanical breakdowns. The LAD unit repaired enough vehicles to move again.*

Those engineers have put in a shift, because despite the endless mechanical delays, by the end of the day the regiment has covered one hundred miles and has set up a temporary camp in Spello. A picturesque and historic town that lies on the southern flank of Mount Subasio. The tractors are parked and tents have been erected on the plain outside the city walls next to the remains of a semi excavated Roman amphitheatre. Although the Germans held the town they withdrew without a fight as they retreated towards Florence and the narrow streets show little sign of the war.

I will accompany my father as he strolls up to the town itself and through the second century *Porta Consolare* with its tall bell tower that has a five-hundred-year-old olive tree on its top. My camera follows him as he walks into the town. The low evening sun lights up the Romanesque façade of the church of Santa Maria Maggiore. Since he is starring in my imaginary film, I can follow him as he gazes up at the *Perugino* frescoes. He will not have seen *The English Patient*, but I have and as I film him wandering up the deserted chancel and into the Baglioni Chapel where he may or may not recognise the exquisite Pinturicchio frescoes showing an *Annunciation, a Nativity and a Dispute with the Doctors,* I feel I am filming in the footsteps of Anthony Minghella.

The next day the convoy assembles in the early dawn and continues its journey northwards. The road is narrow, dusty and badly cratered. I am familiar with the landscape My camera is rolling as they drive up past Perugia and round Lake Trasimene but the view from my father's cab is obscured by the thick pall of dust thrown up by the vehicles in front. I have driven this route on many Umbrian holidays so I have a good idea of what he is missing. The Germans have done their best to slow down the British advance. All the bridges have been blown and our engineers have had to install Bailey bridges.

Those bridges will I know carry the hundreds of vehicles that transport 1st Division going north and 4th Division coming south. And it's not the makeshift bridges that prove to be a problem as the two divisions change places on the front line. Although my camera has a wide-angle lens which will give the impression of a wider thoroughfare, it is obvious that the road is barely able to take two vehicles passing. I can hear my father cursing as our convoy is brought to a standstill to let past a 4th Division convoy with tanks on their wide transporter vehicles being taken back to Rome.

Scene 2: A Room With A View

It is now the middle of August and 19th Field Regiment have set up base outside the tiny hamlet of Pian dei Cerri just a few miles southwest of the Ponte Vecchio. Although there has been a lot of progress to the east of Florence and troops have crossed the Arno, 1st Division are facing a lot more opposition as they try to take the western side of the city. The infantry needs artillery support as they are being harassed by enemy mortars.

When I catch up with my father he is once again in an observation post on a hillside about a mile to the north of the gun emplacements. But this OP is a far cry from the cramped dangerous tunnel next to the Flyover on the Anzio Beach Head. Using his rudimentary Italian and his appealing smile, both of which stood him in good stead during his escape, he has charmed the local farmer to let him and his two signallers set up in the top bedroom of the farmhouse. He has a fine view over the German positions and what is even better, the farmer's wife has brought up some bread, cheese and a bottle of rough red wine. As a film maker and ghost as well, I must ignore the victuals and concentrate on watching my father who has the microphone of the regimental net in his hand. His voice tells me that he is not happy. I know that tone, he was not a serial complainer but when frustrated his voice would harden. As a boy I learnt to steer clear when I heard it.

"I've explained. I can see the mortars and they are giving the KDG[15] a lot of stick. I've got the coordinates and we could take them out, but the blighters are about three hundred metres from the Abbazi Di Salvatore[16]"

"Sorry Drew, no can do. You know the drill. We've got to steer clear of the historical buildings. Give them a wide berth. At least four hundred metres. Abbazi Di Salvatore is on the list.'[17].

[15.] Kings Dragoon Guards, an armoured car reconnaissance regiment.
[16.] The Abbati Santi Salvatore e Lorenzo a Settimo is a stunning example of medieval architecture. The abbey, dating back to the 12th century, is a treasure trove of history and art. The frescoes are a true masterpiece, adorned with intricate details and vibrant colours.
[17.] It was decided that the historic buildings in and around Florence had to be protected. It was believed that if there was any excuse the Germans would show no regard for the importance of ancient monuments and any damage would be blamed on the allies. As a result, the rule was no artillery action within 400 metres of a building of historical importance.

"I could try 'a close shoot.'[18]

"That won't work either. As I explained, I've already referred it to RHQ and suggested a close shoot"

"What about Divisional HQ. Surely, they would see sense. Our chaps are getting a pasting. I am sure we can hit the mortars and go nowhere near the damned Abbazi."

"We've tried Divisional HQ and the response was the same. So you'll have to leave it I'm afraid."

My father is not happy. I watch as he peers through his binoculars. He is watching the men of the Kings Royal Dragoons turning back from their mission. He can see the flash as the mortars fire into the air and then the puff of smoke and debris as they land amongst the retreating armoured cars. It takes seconds before the sound reaches us. But he remembers that sound from his days on the Beach Head and he has a strong sense of the damage they can cause. He may have enjoyed the frescoes in Spello but he was not happy when at the regimental briefing in anticipation of action around Florence, they had been given a map on which an art expert had identified all the buildings deemed to contain artistic treasures and drawn a four hundred metre 'no fire' circle around each one.

If I had a camera with a zoom lens I could have scanned the length of the Arno where every bridge had been destroyed by

---

[18.] The 'close shoot' was a technique whereby the first shells would be aimed just short of the target and then corrected by increments to insure greater accuracy. In this case my father would use the technique to make sure there was no danger to the Abbazia.

the retreating Germans. Just one remained. The Germans too had some sense of historical significance: the Ponte Vecchio had been spared.

Scene Three: Those Damned Mountains August 1944

I need my twenty first century drone again. It is near the end of August 1944 and 1st Division have played their part in clearing the German 14th Army out of Florence and the surrounding area. They had pulled back to their defensive positions in the hills north east of Florence. I call them hills because as my drone begins its journey following 19th Field Regiment, we are travelling over well-tended agricultural land, flat and easy to move across despite the mines and general destruction left by the retreating enemy. But it is not long before the drone is getting closer to those 'hills' and they do not look like hills anymore. They rise to over three thousand feet in less than four miles and they are steep. Very steep with the tops covered in thick forest. This is where the German *16th Panzergrenadier-division* and the *362 Infanterie-division* are dug in. The drone cannot see the full extent of those defences but there were a series of concrete redoubts that had been built by local, virtually slave, labour. The concrete had been made locally but the workers aware of the purpose it was being put to had modified the ingredients so has to make poor quality material that would give little protection if fired upon. A clever piece of resistance that helped even the odds in the Allies' favour.

Today my father is in the leading gun tractor and as the

convoy gets closer to the mountains he recognises the way the Apennine mountains that rise up from the plains and gentle foothills quickly turn into steep peaks. Although his escape took him up into the Eastern mountains the same pattern was repeated and over the next few days he will be reminded of those precipitous slopes with no easy way up. And today as 1st Division start on their mission to push the enemy back as far as the target town of Borgo San Lorenzo, my father understands better than most the challenges that lie ahead. And, although he was at risk as he made his way through the mountains on foot, he was not being attacked at every turn by enemy mortars.

96/97 battery were told to set up a firing position to support the 1st Battalion of the Hertfordshire Regiment as they move to attack the first of the embedded enemy defences. But as for so much of the access to these killing slopes, the tracks were few and far between. They were never intended to take any kind of mechanical vehicle. Farmers up here walked with their life stock and supplies. Whilst the redoubtable Jeep could go almost anywhere, even that ubiquitous American made workhorse with its maximum gradient ability of sixty degrees was defeated by the high Apennines. And it wasn't just the transport that was becoming increasingly difficult. The steep slopes of the mountains, made it harder and harder to find gun positions that could reach the enemy defences.

In trying to find workable locations for the gun placements it was clear that once the infantry moved into the next valley, it would be almost impossible to get the shells over the peaks. The problem was a twenty-five pounder had only limited inclination and the issue was 'crest clearance'. If the crest of the mountain was higher than the parabolic flight path of the shell, the shell would hit the slope and explodes well short of the target on the other side. You can keep raising the angle of the gun up to forty five degrees, but even that wasn't clearing the crest.

To overcome the problem, my father is supervising his battery as they dig the guns in on a slope. If the back of the gun was another twenty degrees lower than the front then that gave a higher parabola and the ability to clear the crest. But it was a high-risk strategy. And his gunners 96/97 battery knew it.

"If we go any lower sir, the recoil will send us back down the valley".

"I know what you mean but I think we can get another few degrees. Keep digging. Just bed the limber in as deep as you can."

"Yes sir. It should be alright while it stays dry, but if it starts to rain and it turns into mud then . . .

"We'll cross that bridge when we come to it."

And it wasn't long before that bridge had to be crossed.

Scene Four: Dirty Weather

On the night of the 28/29th September the rains came: a torrential downpour continued for forty-eight hours. And that was just the start: the heavy rain continued relentlessly for the next six weeks. At the end of September, 96/97 battery had been providing supporting fire for the 1st Hertfordshire Regiment as they fought their way up Monte Toncane. The gun pits and the slit trenches quickly filled up with water and as predicted, those guns with limbers dug deep to achieve the higher angle to clear the crests began to slip back from the recoil. Gunners were up to their knees in water and mud as they desperately shifted the sludge to provide extra support. The rain kept coming. The waterproof capes gave some protection but legs and feet were permanently soaked and cold. Already some were showing signs of trench foot. And yet the guns kept firing.

The infantry battalions were facing obstinate resistance from Germans who were heavily entrenched on the razor-backed high ridges. The approach up the steep and slippery slopes was treacherous. The Germans were able to rain down fire from machine guns and mortars. The infantry needed artillery support. And the gunners of 96/97 Battery along with the rest of 19th Field Regiment were doing their best to target the enemy strongholds and disrupt their deadly purpose. The challenge for the FOOs was that in the chaos of a prolonged assault up the precipitous slopes it was impossible to gauge the speed of advance. One company might make progress whilst another company got bogged down by the terrain or enemy fire. It was up to my father and his colleagues in the OPs to make sure that their fire power never came close to falling on their own attacking infantry. There was enough carnage up on those slopes without the risk of being hit by your own artillery.

★ ★ ★ ★

It is the 29th of September and my father is preparing to leave HQ and head up into the mountains. It is raining. Hard. My father has on a cape that keeps the most of the rain off his body but flaps around his thighs. He is getting wet and he hasn't even begun his journey up the mountainside to his observation post (OP). His signallers are loading their equipment onto the back of a mule. The regimental Jeeps cannot even get up to HQ leave alone take them further up the mountain. The muleteer is from the Punjab[19] and is making no fuss as they load up the two wireless sets, a box of rations and several bulky rolls of cable that will be run out behind them.

Eventually they set off across the hillside. The mule is sure footed but my father is finding that already he is slipping in the mud which coats his boots and gaiters. He knows that since the rains came FOOs have struggled to get into position in a timely fashion, delaying the provision of the artillery support the embattled infantry need. The signallers are running out the cable which they try to lodge behind rocks and tree stumps, off the track. They know that these lines are horribly vulnerable to mortar fire, the boots of men and most commonly the hooves of the mules which are passing up and down what is left of the tracks. The signallers would have hoped to keep contact via wireless but the vertiginous terrain blocks signals in much the same way as my mobile signal would fail me up here. But I am not looking to communicate only observe.

The ground has deteriorated. Where once there were rocks and stones laid down by the farmer providing some stability,

---

[19.] Indian troops played an important role in the Italy campaign, both as combat troops and in a logistical role managing the mules which were the only form of transport in the mountains.

1944

now the track has turned into a stream and even the mule is staggering. The radios slip and their wax cloth covering opens one of them up to the elements. A wet radio is a useless radio. The signallers move quickly to replace the covering. The muleteer offers reassurance to his charge with a low Punjabi chant. My father is up ahead. He strides on. The signallers find it hard to keep up. I am reminded of his time just a year ago, walking on the other side of these same mountains. He was always far ahead of his companion and even when he did stop to rest, by the time Douglas had caught up and was himself ready for a rest, my father was up and off. He was a leader and knew he must keep in contact with his men, but found it hard to curtail his onward propulsion.

Two hours later my father's pace quickens: he can see the farm house ruins through the mist. There is some protection from the wind but the roof has long gone. There will be no protection from the rain. They unload the kit as my father explores the derelict buildings. He needs to be able to see down into the valley where the Hertfordshire infantry are working their way up towards the crest of Monte Tocane. None of the windows give him the vista he requires. He spots what he hopes will give him a viewpoint. It is the crumbling end wall of the ruined barn. It is precarious. The stones are slippery with moss made treacherous by the rain. But he is determined and impulsive. He gets halfway up then slips back and I hear a curse, then a more cautious approach using some fallen beams as a ladder gets him up onto a remnant of the wooden ceiling. He can even lie down and look out through the opening that once led to the dovecot.

My father is soaked through. It is hard to focus his binoculars with the rain dripping down his face and across the lenses. No sooner had he wiped them clear than his view is again distorted by the almost horizontal rain. He hears the familiar whirr of the Spandau machine guns and the thrump of the mortars and he can see the way they land amongst the men of the 1st Hertfordshire as they advance below him. He knows that they too will be staggering through the mud and slipping on the steep slope just as he was on the journey up. If they are visible to my father then they are easy targets for the Germans. He can see where the German machine gunners are dug in and as he finally identifies the coordinates, he starts to shout them down to the signallers below who repeat them out loud before passing them on. A few minutes later, to his and my relief the shells arrive from 96/97 battery. They are close but not close enough and he adjusts the coordinates accordingly. The signallers relay them on and the next salvo lands right on target. The machine gun fire subsides for the time being at least and there is a terse message of appreciation on the Hertfordshire radio. I am proud of my father

Despite the deluge and the water-logged gun pits, 96/97 were able to deliver the high intensity fire that has been ordered by Regimental Head Quarters: "Thirty minutes. Rate Normal" or ninety rounds per gun per day. An impressive rate of fire given that access to the guns had been waterlogged and the track washed away, leaving just enough room to carry up the twenty-five pound shells a mile up from the valley floor by hand and in single file. And thanks to the feedback from my father and the other two FOOs out on the mountainside, most of those ninety shells were landing on target. And by the end of the second day the Hertfordshire regiment had reached the summit of Monte Tacone and the enemy was in retreat.

It is two days later, up on the muddy slopes above the guns my father's observation team are slipping and sliding their way back down towards the gun emplacements.

My father, his two signallers and the muleteer are barely recognizable: their uniforms caked in filth, their boots heavy with accumulated mud. Even the mule is having trouble staying upright and its minder Kuldeep is straining on the reins to stop it from falling as the load of radios cable and what is left of the supplies swing from side to side. As they pass by guns my father smiles weakly as he acknowledges the ironic "Wet enough for you sir!". He would usually be happy to join in the banter, but he is exhausted and desperate to find some shelter and a cup of hot tea. He has been up on the mountain exposed to the elements for three long days.

My father crawls into his tent, twists and contorts his stiff body out of his wet clothes and pulls on a dry set and then pulls a couple of blankets around himself. He is curling up on his rocking camp bed: a foetal coil in search of some inner heat. He takes out his false teeth and shortly afterwards his head hits the makeshift pillow. He is asleep and I slip away back to the twenty first century: to central heating, thermal underwear and the beguiling warmth of climate change.

Scene Five: A White Christmas

There was some snow at the end of November but it melted away after a few days. The serious stuff fell just before Christmas. That first fall had coincided with the issue of special winter clothing. I am filming my father as he is dressing for yet another excursion up the mountain to take over an OP from his colleague from 67th Field Regiment. He has already put on his long woollen pants and is now pulling a string vest over his head. I remember when the string vest was a fashion statement in the sixties but also understand how they could provide a layer of odd- feeling pockets of warmth against the skin. Then he puts on his shirt, a khaki pullover, his battle dress tunic, a leather jerkin and then his army great coat. Outside his tent he puts on a white balaclava and pulls on the white smock and pyjama style trousers, all part of his snow camouflage.

If I was able to interview him, I might have asked if that lot was going to keep him warm in the OP. I am fairly certain he would have replied:

"It works for a while and its damned sweaty walking up there, but sitting still in that wind, the cold seeps in and overnight it's bloody freezing. And the worst part is trying to keep your feet warm."

Whilst the issue of cold weather clothing did make a difference both in terms of visibility and warmth, the army could not solve the problems cause by wet and cold feet. The heavy army boots were not waterproof and soaked up water. Once wet it was a nightmare to get them dry. They experimented with rubber Wellington boots especially for gunners standing in flooded gun pits. But as I know all too well, the rubber boot is fiendishly cold and get sucked off going through thick mud. When my father arrived back from OP duty with feet that had been wet and cold for a couple of days, I film him taking his socks off, trying to rub some feeling back into his feet and putting on a pair of dry socks and stuffing the wet socks into his battledress under the arm pits hoping his body heat, such as there was, would dry them out. But despite their best efforts trench foot was a constant threat. Nobody wanted to see their toes go black.

The heavy snow fell overnight on the 23th and 24th December, although there is nothing nostalgic about a white Christmas. No turkeys have been killed nor is there plum pudding on the way. There might have been some enhanced rations with a Christmas flavour on offer, but the snow fall has made the roads impassable. On December 24th, there was less concern about getting food supplies and Christmas goodies up to the valley HQs and rather more concern with how to evacuate the wounded. All available troops were organised into clearance gangs working to clear the snow drifts on the access roads.

When Christmas Day dawned, there was little sign of celebration and yet all units received the order only to fire if the enemy fired first and they did not fire. There was, it seemed, an unofficial truce observed by both sides. For a time, it looked as if one of the infantry regiments had broken the truce, but it turned out that the Vickers machine guns were seizing up in the freezing cold. The only way to keep them working was to fire them every day. On Christmas Day, they were fired into the air. The Germans surprised everyone by ringing the church bells of the *Chiesa di San Salvatore* in Vedriano a village a few miles to the East of our position. This surprised the gunners as they were convinced they had destroyed most of the village and the church.

My father is walking back from the quartermaster's store. He is carrying four bottles under his arm. He arrives at the gun placements where the gunners are crouched round an improvised fire grate. They have an open box of the usual fourteen-man compo rations and by way of a treat they have mixed up the two tins of steak and kidney with the four tins of baked beans and added the three tins of spam: the unappetizing mess is starting to bubble away. They look up as my father joins the group.

"What have you got there sir? We were hoping for roast turkey and stuffing"

"Sorry chaps. Best I can do is a double ration of rum."

"That'll do sir. Give us a minute. We left the best glasses in the front room cabinet."

There is a burst of enthusiasm as men search for the tin mugs and line up for a double tot. It is an orderly crew.

"Happy Christmas sir. What do you think? Home by next time?"

"Wish I knew Bombardier. They don't tell me much more than they tell you. You never know what 'the powers that be' have got in store."

In fact, 'the powers that be' did have plans. 1st Division was to be withdrawn from active service in Italy. The final push to finally defeat the Germans was going to be left up to the American 85th Division. There were rumours that the Division might be taken back to the UK, perhaps even disbanded. Word spread that a regimental advanced party had left the camp. Destination unknown. Then in the second week of January the orders came to start packing up. It was easier said than done. The large canvas gun covers had frozen solid: and the tarpaulins that had covered the Command Post were almost impossible to fold up. Eventually the petrified equipment was wrestled into submission and the guns were winched up and out of their flooded emplacements. Finally, the regimental convoy formed up and just after midnight started the perilous journey down the winding narrow roads back towards Florence. The road was clear but fiendishly icy and the hair-pin bends were terrifying. After a twenty hour drive they ended up at their bivouac area near Bivigliano. There they handed in their winter clothing and surplus ammunitions. They were obviously not going back to the mountains.

After two days rest the word reached my father and the rest of 96/97 Battery. They were headed to the Middle East. What I know, but my father does not yet know, is they will be shipped to Palestine and that, in just a month's time, he will meet my mother.

Stoke Newington, London August 2024

Dear Dad,

I am still reeling from how much I have learnt about your time after you returned to your regiment. I know at the end of the film we put the simple sentence: Drew Bethell rejoined his regiment and went on to fight in Italy until the liberation was completed. I must have written those words and yet I never bothered to ask you what they meant. I am ashamed of that. Before I started this journey in search of you, I knew next to nothing about the, often ignored, Italian campaign and yet from the moment you re-joined the regiment at Anzio, you were in the thick of it. You did like to tell a story and, God knows, what happened at Anzio and then in the mountains beyond Florence was worthy of some story telling. And yet you never mentioned it. Once again, I assume that you simply supressed those memories, just like Recce Ridge, Anzio and Dunkirk. I wouldn't blame you.

But now we are at that stage in the story where I can say: "For you the war is over". It is not strictly true as 1st Division could still have been called back to the front line. As you know, the Italian campaign did not finally end until May 1945. When you left the battle was still in full force and it must have seemed that victory was a long way off. So, when the regiment landed at Haifa at the start of February it was still possible that you could return once again to face the Germans in combat. By late 1944 Palestine had been used for resting and re-equipping battle-weary divisions from the Italian front. I am pleased to say that it soon became clear that you would not be going back to Europe; instead you would be involved in peace keeping duties in the growing conflict between the newly arrived Jewish population and the Palestinian Arabs.

I do not want to make light of your involvement in the conflict between the Palestinians and Israelis. As I write this, there is a potentially catastrophic war raging in the Middle East, a brutal, possibly existential conflict that has its roots in the battles over the establishment of an Israeli state which were just beginning to intensify as you arrived. I will get on to investigating the role your regiment played in 'holding the ring' and I do so, I have to confess, with some trepidation. It is eighty years since you played a part in the conflict, and yet the current toxicity does leave me desperate for reassurance that your participation was not complicit in the suppression of the Palestinian cause.

Before going there, I have had to launch a far happier investigation. Neither you nor my mother ever spoke about how you met. I know the bare bones but there is no detail. My very existence depends on a fortuitous meeting and so you will have to excuse a fascination as to the details of just what happened: when and where. Luckily, I have a few clues to work on. I am fairly sure you had no idea that my mother kept all your love letters to her. They are a treasure trove of intimacy and reveal a side of you that has transformed my appreciation of your emotional capacity. It has come as a shock but a delightful one.

But before we get to your letters, I want to focus on Pam Woosnam. I am sure you eventually got to know a lot about what she did in the war: before she met you. Again, I am sad to say that I knew only the bare bones. Luckily, she also left me a heap of the letters she wrote home to her parents, so I have been able to piece together what happened to her. It is an account that reminds me just what a force of nature she was and why you must have fallen for her when you finally did meet just after you landed in Palestine.

Love,

Hum

CHAPTER 17

Pam's Story

Egypt 1943 to 1945

Pam Bethell aged 20

Pamela Mary Woosnam was born on the 6th December 1922 in the mid-Wales town of Builth Wells. Her father Ralph Woosnam owned an estate in the Irfon Valley where he managed four farms and many acres of forestry. Her mother Kathleen came from another landowning family with estates nearby. Her childhood was comfortable, rural and contained. She did go to boarding school in England, but as a seventeen-year-old at the outbreak of war she had a limited experience of the world outside her friends and family in that corner of Wales.

Early in 1941 she joined the Women's Royal Navy Service (WRNS) aged nineteen and was posted to HMS Watchful at Milford Haven where she was trained and engaged in administrative duties related to the war. I can find little record of that time. No letters have been passed down to me. She had no cause to feel overly anxious, her parents were a mere ninety miles away and the war was a lot further away than that. There seemed to be no certainty that she would ever get close to a theatre of war. There was secretarial and administrative work to be done in support of the Royal Navy on active service and the most likely posting would be to Admiralty House in London. But then something happened. The first letter of the numerous letter I do have is written with due deference to the censors who will read every letter she writes for the next three years: there is no date and no detail:

My Darling Mummy and Daddy,

This is just to let you know that I have gone. I don't expect you will hear from me again for a bit. Everything is marvellous and we are all awfully thrilled to be really off at last.

Don't worry at all about me and keep well.

All my love

Pam

I am not sure how reassuring that would have been to Ralph and Kathleen. The combination of mystery and delight could have been both comforting and alarming.

It has taken some detective work and the power of Google search for me to reconstruct what I think happened to her then. I do know from a slew of subsequent letters that she was on board a ship for many weeks. Again, the censors have been diligent: where she was carefree enough to date her letters, the censors have carefully cut out the offending date with a razor. However, it seems that in the middle of February 1943 she boarded the RMS Cape Town Castle, a passenger liner converted into a troop ship. What she did not know, because they were not told, she was heading for Egypt, not via the Mediterranean as that was deemed too dangerous, but via the Cape of Good Hope. It was a journey that took two months to cover almost fourteen thousand miles.

> *My Darlings,*
>
> *Well, here we are- it's very difficult to write because we just don't know how much we are allowed to say! It's not terribly comfortable. We have 18 other people in our cabin and Betts (her close friend from Milford Haven) and I are sleeping on mattresses on the floor. However, it isn't really too bad and we shall soon get used to it.*
>
> *There are quite a few rules we have to keep such as Wrens are not allowed to sunbathe or sleep on deck. Also, we are only allowed NON-Alcoholic drinks!!! Which is a bit unfair as there could be quite a few parties if we were allowed them.*

Despite the lack of alcoholic drinks and uncomfortable sleeping quarters, she seems be having a good time, a few days later she writes:

> *Life continues to be just as good and we are both having a terrific time. We haven't had a dull moment since we got on board which is wonderful because we thought the journey was going to be rather boring*
>
> *The weather is absolutely heavenly not at all too hot. The evenings are simply marvellous, it gets dark pretty early and there's the most wonderful sunset then when its dark there are hundreds and hundreds of stars, I've never seen anything quite like it. I can*

watch the patches of phosphorous in the swell made by the other ships for hours. (Her ship was part of a convoy of some fifteen other ships)

But it's not all plain sailing. Bizarrely, the censors did not catch the date of the next letter, so I know this was February 25th, which means they were most likely off the coast of West Africa prior to landing at Freetown in Sierra Leone:

> It's been a pretty rough day and not many people have stood up to it. We had a life boat drill this morning and everyone <u>had</u> to attend however ill they were feeling. It really was pathetic some of the poor things could hardly stand. We had to stand for ages in lines along the deck and there was a continuous stream of people looking pale green and rushing to the sides. Betty and I had taken our Seoxyl which is <u>marvellous!</u> We're feeling absolutely grand.

Seoxyl was an anti-sea sickness treatment which assures the user on the outside of the packet that it "does not contain Heroin or Cocaine or any other habit-forming drugs".

The next letter comes from a lot further south and indicates that they are well on the way to the next stop, Cape Town.

> We are still plodding along and it's been terribly hot for quite a long time now. Life has been a little trying just lately, as the powers-that-be have taken it

> upon themselves to tighten up our various rules and regulations. We are now not allowed to wear plain clothes at all and have to boil all day in blue skirts and while shirts which in this extreme heat is, to say the least of it, trying!! Also, our deck space has been cut down. We now have very severe boundaries which we are not allowed to cross. It's most unpleasant because by the time all the Wrens and all their boyfriends are packed into one very small bit of deck, it is so crowded one begins to feel suffocated. So Betty and I spend a lot of our time lying on our beds in a very bad temper.

Since I am taking an interest in my parents' early love life, I am wondering how she feels as an innocent twenty-year-old being squeezed off the deck by her colleagues coupled with men who really shouldn't be allowed in the women's space. It seems rather obvious that she had not found a male companion and there must have been a tinge of envy fuelling her bad temper.

A few weeks later the ship has left Durban where they stop off for two days during which she and her friends travel in-land and she ends a lengthy description with: "We did have the most heavenly two days and we shall none of us ever forget them." However, as they set off she is distressed to discover that her best friend Betty has been assigned to a post in Durban and left the ship.

> It was all absolutely shattering and the very last thing we expected, but time was so short we didn't have time to do anything. I tried to complain to our commanding officer but by the time she asked

them to reconsider the drafting officer had arranged everything and it was too late. It's all a bit awfully bad luck but it's no good being miserable now because it is done and we shall have to make the best of it.

We know that everyone on active service in wartime needed to 'get used' to separation from friends and family. My mother is clearly very upset and feels that she might have been able to pull strings but there is an inexorable feeling that the Drafting Officer would hold sway even had she made representation. The bureaucracy of war was a soulless business and it is touching to see my somewhat entitled mother raging against the system.

As the RMS Cape Town Castle makes its way up the east coast of Africa they finally reveal Pam's final destination:

My destination is the very last place in the world I imagined, in fact I wasn't even sure I knew where it was when they told me the name. It's most awfully tantalising not being able to tell you anything about it or where it is.

The next stop is Aden and there is more disappointment although tinged with relief:

Unfortunately, at our last stop I lost my other two friends, which was rather depressing, they have struck a very nasty posting poor dears. I am thankful it wasn't me. Daddy you will know what I mean if I could tell you.

My maternal grandfather must have had some experience of Aden, he spent much of the First World War in the Middle East. It is a port on the extreme west coast of the Yemen and was used as a coaling station for ships going east and north, as a result was known as the "Coalhole of the East".

By the middle of April, she has reached her destination. It is the port of Alexandria on the Mediterranean, some one hundred and fifty miles north of Cairo. She will have travelled the gruelling two hundred miles from the port of Suez by road. She will be working at HMS Nile, the Royal Navy shore base which was located on the Ras el Tin point on the north harbour. A smart part of an ancient and cultured city where the King of Egypt's imposing palace was located. She describes her new posting in a letter to Helen Howland another friend still living in WRNS Quarters in Milford Haven.

> *Well after all my wanderings this where I have landed up. I must say it is the last place I ever thought I should get to and didn't awfully want to come here. But now I'm here I don't really mind it. So far it is actually quite fun in fact I have never known such a round of gaiety! It's almost too hectic.!*
>
> *We are living in a convent which is simply packed with Wrens. We are in a room with 30 beds! We don't really have any rules, not half as many as I was expecting. We have to be in by 10.30 every night with one late pass a week until 12.30.*

> *I can't tell you much about the work, but so far, I've found it absolutely deadly dull. Milford Haven was positively thrilling in comparison. I was amazed as I expected it to be rather exciting.*
>
> *Well my dear I must stop now as I am on night watch and there's some work to do.*

It has been very hard to establish exactly what work she was doing during her time in Egypt. Every letter has been censored and she has obviously learnt not to give anything away. I do know that HMS Nile was an administrative centre for the Mediterranean fleet. I suspect it was indeed rather dreary office work, although she did once mention signals and coding work. I like to think that however bored she was the information she was processing played its part in how the navy supported Montgomery's successful battle to drive Rommel's Afrika Corp out of North Africa. Indeed, she may well have handled signals that coordinated the protection of my father's regiment as they were transported across the Mediterranean to North Africa in April 1943, just after she arrived.

What is very clear from her letters is that she did indeed have a hectic social life. There are regular descriptions of moonlight picnics, tennis and sailing. And then there were the parties. Most letters refer to a party, often several. Then six months after arriving in Alex, she meets a celebrity:

> *I don't think I ever told you about a party I went to last weekend when I met Noel Coward. He has been*

> all round this part of the world doing shows for the troops. It was a terrific thrill to meet him especially as I had just seen his film "In Which we Serve". I had quite a long talk with him and he seemed very charming.

She does not often refer to meeting up with men. A few connections with the family back in Wales.:

> Wasn't it extraordinary my meeting Norman Harrison?! I think being out here must have improved him because he is really quite a nice boy now, and I remember you thinking him rather grim when he came to stay.

I can find not a hint of any romantic interest which is not surprising in letters to her parents, but I did catch an oblique reference that might have indicated something a little more intimate with another young man:

> A friend of mine from the ship flew down to see me the other day. It was a complete surprise and lovely to see him again.

Flying down to see her? Just to catch up on old times on the ship? I don't think I am being overly intrusive in suspecting that there may be more to those few lines than meets the eye.

What is clear from her letters is that despite her restricted rural background with limited experience of the world outside her mid-Wales home, Pam was gifted with the travel gene.

Although it took her a while to get used to life in Alexandria, it was not long before she and her friend Peggy had plans for their seven day leave in December 1943:

> *Our latest plan for our leave is to go to Beirut for the first few days then have a quick look at Syria, then we shall go down to Jerusalem for the last two days. It's rather a lot but I hope we shall be able to do it all – seven days is so very short!!*

In fact, they abandoned the Beirut and Syria parts of the plan and sensibly decided to spend their seven days in Jerusalem. It was gruelling twenty-six-hour train journey to get there. The final eight hours on a train through Palestine was clearly a challenge:

> *I have never seen anything so disgustingly dirty in all my life! It could only just stagger along and whenever we came to a hill half the passengers had to get out and almost push it up!!!*

In contrast to the train getting there, the friends did not hang about once they arrived in Jerusalem. There is an eleven-page letter home describing in great detail visits to: The Wailing Wall, the Garden Tomb, Calvary and the Church of the Holy Sepulchre. That was just the first day! On the next day a friendly Brigadier drove them through the mountains and down to Gaza 'the place where Samson pushed over pillars and played around with Delilah'. She found it just 'a dirty little village' with little to recommend it. I can only wonder what she would have made of the twenty-first century fate of the area to which that little village gave its name. They managed to get to Nazareth, Tiberias by the sea of Galilee and to Haifa. She writes lyrically about the scenery and feels they had a pretty thorough tour of the "best parts of Palestine".

As I write this it is hard to imagine a Palestine or Jerusalem that was so accessible to a couple of well-brought-up but unworldly English girls. She is unnervingly baffled by the Orthodox Jews she sees in Jerusalem with *"their funny hats and little locks of hair"*. She also writes a lot about the poverty she encounters: *"It is hard to believe people can live like that!"* I like to think she would have felt guilty about her lack of cultural and economic empathy. And yet I can only admire her confidence and curiosity in an alien environment. It was a quality that developed into a wander-lust that drove her throughout her adult life. She was to grow an inveterate traveller well into her eighties. And I have to remember that on the train back to Alexandria she celebrated her birthday. She was just twenty one and the only present she received on the day was a large Jaffa orange which Peggy plucked from a passing tree as the train trundled slowly through an orange grove.

September 13th 1943

We took this photo when Peggy and I went out to El Alamein with Hubert Alfrey. We are standing by one of the German tanks that were captured in battle. There is a sort of park there with all the hundreds of enemy tanks and every kind of vehicle. It was the most amazing sight and awfully interesting to look at them and compare them with some of our tanks that had also been shot up and were there too. The heaviest and best tanks the Germans used didn't look a patch on our Shermans. Of course, Hubert knew all about it. He had been there for the battle.

The Second Battle of El Alamein took place almost exactly a year earlier and was seen as a critical turning point in the war. It was the last throw of the dice for the allies as Rommel and the Afrika Corps were getting very close to taking control of Egypt and more importantly the Suez Canal. The village of El Alamein that gave the battle its name is on the coast sixty miles west of Alexandria. The battle raged over the fifty miles due south down to the impenetrable Qattara Depression. The tank graveyard that Peggy and Pam visited stood as testimony to the heavy losses in men and equipment on both sides. It was touch-and-go and took over two weeks of attrition before the allies could claim a significant victory. That's the history. What strikes me, looking at that photo is how very attractive those two young women seem, dressed in the 'whites' that constituted the Wren uniform once the heat arrived. Hubert lounges across the flank of the Marder 135 Half-track tank that once belonged to the now retreating 221st Panzer Division. His proprietorial air seems to apply equally to the enemy tank and his two lovely companions.

Later in the same letter she writes:

> We had a terrific party to celebrate the Italians giving in and consumed an immense amount of champagne. Of course, some had to be kept for the Germans and the Japs! (sic). I am sure it won't be too long before it is all over now and one really feels that one can look forward to coming home to no war.

Sadly, that was wishful thinking. It was to be another two years before she eventually returned home to 'no war'. However, what she was unaware of, was that on almost the same day she visited El Alamein, a young artillery officer was also benefiting from the Italian armistice and was setting off on his journey up into the Apennines. And he had another 18 months of active wartime service before he was to meet the love of his life.

After three years it seems that she is in line for promotion. She becomes a Leading Wren almost as soon as she arrives in Egypt. Then in May 1944 she writes;

> *I have just been told I have reached the giddy heights of Petty Officer. Not at all exciting really it only entails a few brass buttons and a different hat! Personally, I think it is very little consolation after three and a half years 'stooging'. One merely becomes a prefect in the "kindergarten" – it doesn't let one out of it altogether! However, I suppose it can't last forever!*

And indeed, it does not last forever. Three months later she writes about being close to finishing a course that will cause her to be commissioned as an officer:

> *We are just finishing the course at the moment and when we've done our exams and got into the uniform of Third Officer – then the fun begins!! I have a decided feeling in my bones that they will shoot me off somewhere because they are rather against one staying in the same place with a commission. I think Italy would be rather fun for my last six months, however I think the war will be over before that. Everyone here gives it three months.*

She had her eye on a posting to the naval base at Naples, but it was not to be. In August she writes about her new posting:

> The course is now over and I am a full blown Third Officer. I have been appointed to a new job, which as you see will means my working in Cairo. I don't know anything about it because it's frightfully "hush hush" and they won't tell me a thing until I start. I went for an interview and my boss, who is a Squadron Leader in the RAF, said that for this particular job they are very fussy and he has to signal to London to give them time there to find out all about me, whether I have any Germans in the family etc!!

As with my father, the more I look into this, the more distressed I become. I so regret my failure to talk to my mother about her work in Egypt and most especially her 'hush hush' work in Cairo. It must have been a lot more serious than the admin work she was doing in Alexandria to require further vetting by the security services in London. What I do know is that the North Africa Campaign and the naval activity in the Mediterranean were greatly helped by signal intercepts that came from Bletchley Park and the breaking of the Enigma Code using Alan Turing's decoding device, 'the Bombe'. These intercepts were sent to the various theatres of war, via our own encryption systems. It was essential to keep the source of the Enigma material hidden from the Germans so those handling it must have required a high level of security clearance. On the basis of her vetting experience it is not fanciful to surmise that she was decrypting and encrypting those most secret signals.

1943-1945

As with so many women in the Second World War, it looks as if my mother was working at a level of intellectual and technical competence that she never utilised during the rest of her adult life. I knew she was an intelligent woman who was capable of so much but who subsequently never appeared to aspire to be anything more than to be a good wife to my father and a loving mother to her children. And yet I feel proud that for a short time, at least, she was given the opportunity to show her capability and potential, even if she probably did not appreciate it at the time.

I have found it almost impossible not to speculate about my mother's relationship with the opposite sex during these three years. It was a situation where the men, who so out-numbered the women, and were far away from their own familial constraints, must have taken a carnal interest in these young women. I have read the *Levant Trilogy* by Olivia Manning which deals with the social lives of exactly the same class of men and women in Cairo and Alexandria during the same period. In her telling there was no lack of sexual encounters. As for Pam, the only testimony I have comes in letters to her mother and father. There is no hint of anything other than what she describes as "gaiety": midnight swimming parties on the beach, dancing all night and meeting men for lengthy drinking sessions in the Club. I feel much as my daughter does who, when she spoke to her grandmother about her war and the two-month voyage around Africa, asked "Did you really not kiss any of the two thousand men on that ship?" To which her grandmother replied "No absolutely not. They were gentlemen!" Although my daughter claims there was a twinkle in her eye.

However, we have now arrived at the next stage of the story when romance is in the air. As early as November 1944 when my father was still on Monte Grande, my mother writes about a planned holiday in early February:

> *We have now decided to get up a party of six of seven of us and go and have a week's skiing in the mountains of Lebanon – apparently, it's just like Switzerland and a perfect place for a holiday. It should be great fun.*

Then on the 7th of February 1945 she writes:

> *Elizabeth and I are flying up to Syria on Saturday. For our leave. Her boss has a flat in Beirut, so we shall stay there for a couple of days then go up to a hotel in the mountains to do some skiing. I shall probably break my neck never having done it before but it will be fun.*

What she doesn't know is by that time, a young artillery officer in the 19th Field Regiment has just arrived in Palestine from Italy and has been given a week's leave starting on Saturday the 12th February. The rest of his friends have gone to Alexandria, but he fancies a bit of skiing too and is also heading up to that hotel in the mountains of Lebanon.

Stoke Newington, London September 2024

Dear Dad,

I know you will recognise that intrepid and independent young woman. I can certainly see why she might have attracted you. So, to see how you reacted to her I am going to turn to your love letters. I felt a little queasy about trawling through those intimate missives and I cannot imagine myself publishing quotations from them whilst you were alive. You would have been embarrassed and I suspect even angry at such a betrayal. So how come I feel able to exploit your intimacies some thirty years after your death? Well, the main reason is that those letters reveal a part of you that was mostly invisible to me and to your close family, let alone your friends and colleagues. Your obituary in the Journal of the Royal Artillery included the sentence: 'He had great style and many friends but something in him would never let them get too close". All those friends are dead now, but I am certain that, had they the chance to read some of these intensely loving letters, they would have thought better of you not worse. So, I am confident in the knowledge that those of us that are still alive and the generations to come will see you for the sensitive and loving man you so clearly were.

Sadly, I only have one side of the correspondence, my mother's voice is absent, but her presence is deeply felt. It is a wonderfully *romantic story and even though there are some blank spots where I can only surmise, there is enough evidence to construct a narrative that I hope would meet with both your and mum's approval.*

I shall begin by trying to work out just what happened during the seven days between Monday 11th of February and Sunday 17th, the week that both you and Pam spent at The Palace Hotel, Bacarré, across from the Cedars of Lebanon. I know it was a chance encounter but it turned into so much more. By the end of that week, you were infatuated with each other: it was the origin story of your love affair that lasted for the next eighteen months and resulted in your marriage and eventually in my conception.

With love,

Hum

CHAPTER 18

Falling in love

Palestine 1945

19th Field Regiment: Regimental Diary February 1945

2nd Feb	*Main body of regiment disembarked HMT MARIGOT at HAIFA, PALESTINE and proceeded to Camp 87, PARDES HANNA, near HADERA.*
12th Feb	*Leave party of approx. 300 departed HADERA Railway Station for ALEXANDRIA.*
19th Feb	*Leave party return to camp.*

The regimental record is overly concise. There is little to go on and yet the 12th February is a significant date for me. Although it records that all three hundred members of the regiment set off to enjoy their leave in Alexandria, I know that Drew Bethell bucked the trend. He fancied a bit of skiing and he and a few friends headed north to the Cedars of Lebanon. I will discover in a later letter that he first met Pam Woosnam on the same day because she too was on her way to the same hotel. I have to piece together what happened but her letter to her parents a few days after she gets back suggests she had a good time.

> 22nd February 1945
>
> My darlings,
>
> I hope you haven't been worrying because you haven't heard from me, I'm sorry about it but I've been away on leave since the 10th and only got back here yesterday.
>
> We had an absolutely heavenly time up in the mountains, we stayed at a killing little hotel right at the top and skied absolutely all and every day. The weather was glorious. We skied all day in aertex shirt and trousers, no woollies or anything. The only thing was the sun was so terrifically hot that we all got burned to cinders, all the skin came off and I look an awful sight now!! However, I never felt so fit. One seemed to have endless energy, we used to start off skiing at about seven every morning, go on til it got dark and then danced for quite half the night and still not feel a bit tired, it was quite amazing. We took about eight rolls of film so I shall have lots of photos to show you when we get home.

I have the album in which she stuck a selection of those photos each with a carefully written caption. They are grainy black and white and about two inches by two inches. In most it is hard to see the features of the chums she has so carefully identified. But there is one name that appears several times: Drew, my father. If I combine the evidence from her breathless account with the photos of Drew, I feel I can say with some confidence that the 'marvellous feeling' and the 'endless energy' came from the fact that she had fallen in love.

Two Wogs - Self and Drew

BETHELL PASHA

These don't give much away (except a regrettable racist descriptor) and yet there he is clearly labelled. Evidence of his presence and indirectly of my mother's intense interest in him. There is one other picture of the two of them where it is easy to identify them and yet it is enigmatic in its meaning. Underneath she has written: SELF AND DREW: LOOKING PEEVISH!

I have interrogated that picture at length. It stands out. Every other picture is consensual and illustrates the fun they are having: skiing, sitting in the snow or falling over. This is taken in the car park of the hotel, and is messy and unromantic. Their expressions are ambiguous. They could be an established couple with my father putting on a face for the photo and my mother grimacing at his assertive presence. Were they really 'peevish'? Had they had a row at this very early stage in their relationship? Or maybe this was taken before the romantic sparks had flown. They certainly do not look as if they are in love. And the truth is I have no evidence from my mother that they were in love. Apart from that effusive letter written the day after she arrives back from leave, the only letters from which to draw a firmer conclusion that she has fallen for this man are letters from the man himself, written after they had parted company. I have looked in vain for the letter in which my mother writes to her parents telling them that she has found a man. Throughout her previous correspondence she refers to various friends who have got engaged or married. She displays a not very well disguised envy. As it happens, shortly after she fell in love, she returned to England and would have been able to tell her parents in person.

If I want to follow my parents' romance from that first meeting on the slopes, then I must move across to that large bundle of letters my father wrote to my mother in the following eighteen months. He had to write because, as we will see, they will be apart for many months. He was a prolific correspondent. At least five letters a week, filling the page with his tiny tidy handwriting. They will be my guide. If my mother's letters reinforced what I already knew and loved about her, my father's letters reveal a side to him that comes as a total revelation. Sadly, I have none of her letters to him. As far as I can tell he did not keep them: perhaps he was embarrassed by them. But I know she wrote to him, almost as frequently because he refers to her letters and the joy they gave him. He answers her queries and responds to her reciprocal expressions of love and longing.

The first letter I have is dated 20th February the day after he and Pam parted.

> *Pam my darling,*
>
> *It was marvellous to have the reprieve of the sentence of not seeing you again – and it was a perfect evening from me because I was with you, but I still wish we could have gone to places that were not quite so beastly. But God willing we may be able to do that on Saturday evening.*

From later correspondence I have worked out that he drove Pam down the mountain from Becharée to Lydda RAF base some fifteen miles south of Tel Aviv where she was meant to catch a plane back to Cairo. Somehow, they either missed the plane or it was cancelled. It meant that they had to spend the evening together. That was the reprieve. It looks as if they were stuck on the base which can have had few places for a young couple wanting some privacy to make the best of their surprise extra evening together. They stayed up late but eventually she had to leave him and go to her temporary bed:

> *What was the reaction of the RAF to the Wren officer clocking back into her billet at such a late hour?*

He had to drive back to his regiment in Camp 87 Pardes some fifty miles further south. It did not go well:

The journey back last night was a blood-stained episode – metaphorically that is. We followed the alleged straight road which entailed a diversion of about forty miles – it rained – and all that piling up on the fact that I did not want to admit to myself that it might be our last evening together made the general attitude to life this morning what one might call "bloody minded".

It seems that she is destined to leave for England in the next week. She is to travel home by ship from Alexandria. However, he is hoping to have one last evening with her and thinks he can swing it to escape from his regiment and cadge a lift from the RAF to fly him down for a fleeting visit over the next weekend before she departs.

Darling- it would be so much better to say it rather than write it – don't let "Them" lock you up in some awful transit camp until the boat goes, or is there still some chance that you may not go at all. Life would immediately assume a bright rosy shade, as opposed to rather dull grey, only illuminated by the thought that this Saturday in Cairo is still a better than fifty-fifty chance.

Apparently, he had spoken to the Adjutant who said he could leave on Saturday morning as long as he was back by Sunday evening.

The next letter is dated February 26th, a week later and that dash for a night in Cairo with his 'darling' was not to be. The weather intervened and Pam is on her way home:

"They are playing "It's Foolish but it's Fun" [20] *It's one of our tunes but then there's the awful thought that you left this morning.*

Oh, sweetheart, I got your letter this evening and nearly wept, most ignominious, but it's true. You left this morning and I can't do anything about seeing you now I feel rather empty and hopeless. So long to wait until I can watch you smile again and dance with you – not the dance of the rabble- but with you darling, miles above and away from them all. And the something in your hair that made me rather foolish. You always said it was plain shampoo and I still can't believe it. A week ago, today I was sufficiently conceited to think that Cairo was a certainty, darling it was, but that damned weather spoilt it. Now you have gone and despite all the self-consoling I do, all I can think of is you, my sweet, on some boat going further away every moment.

[20.] Recorded in 1941 by Deana Durbin :
I love to climb an apple tree
Though apples green are bad for me
And I'll be sick as I can be
It's foolish but it's fun

1945

It is just two weeks since he bumped into my mother at the Palace Hotel and they are clearly in love. I cannot stop myself from imagining quite what happened when he became "rather foolish". I look back at those photos of them skiing and my mother's letter describing how she skied all day and danced most of the night and I am wondering at what point did they fall for each other. Was his moment of 'foolishness' a passionate kiss? Did they go further? And, how did they know that this wasn't just some holiday fling. I can reveal that they are not going to see each other for another eleven months and yet something happened which lit a flame that would burn bright, fuelled merely by the written word. I wonder whether the intensity of their connection was typical for a generation that had been largely kept apart by war. Starved of the company of women, the men must have been absurdly quick to build romantic castles in the air based on an evening of passion. Yet, how could Pam and Drew possibly have known that this was going to be the one after just a few days on the ski slopes and nights on the dance floor?

Most of all, I am astounded by the revelation of this tender passionate man. A twenty-four-year-old public-school boy who went to war at the age of nineteen and has been living in male company ever since. He is a product of his time: the man who said to me "One was brought up not to talk about oneself". And yet this one woman has caused him to lose his vulnerability and open his heart and pour out his love and devotion onto the page. As we will see he becomes aware that writing is one thing but saying something out loud is a very different matter and as he prepares to meet his lover again, we will see that awareness turn into trepidation. But for the time being there is little restraint in his profession of love and longing. I do not recognise this man and yet I am thrilled to have discovered him.

In his next letter, a week later, we learn that he has damaged his knee playing rugger and what seemed a simple bruise has turned into something more serious and he is in hospital. It gives him time for further reflection:

Pam Darling mine,

This is the second evening in hospital. It's bloody. I just have nothing to do but lie here and write letters. If I start to think I start remembering the leave, the journey back, that last evening together – so many memories and yet so few-so little time and yet so much happened. My souvenirs of those last few days are so many: walking back from the Club when the sun was setting and the feeling of being at peace with the world in general and having you sweetheart. There are so many places I want to do and show you. I want to watch your smile and watch you in a serious mood. That was the evening we had dinner at Mon Repos. The next one, you will wear the same red evening dress and we will dine at the Berkeley, or one of those corner tables in Hatchett's[21].

[21.] Hatchett's was a famous London restaurant with night club attached. It had stood on its location 66-68 Piccadilly since the late 19th Century

Later in the same letter he suddenly realises she may be in some danger:

> *I read a thing in the papers the day before yesterday about there is a submarine offensive in the Atlantic. My dear if you are reading this it won't have mattered, but the imagination when it's got nothing better to do, runs over all the hideous things that could happen.*

He was right to be worried, even at that late stage of the war German U boats were still operating in the North Atlantic. However, he would have been relieved to know that her ship reached Liverpool unscathed. A few days later Pam was reunited with her parents.

CHAPTER 19
Getting to Know You

Palestine. February 1945.

It's now two weeks after Pam and Drew first met. He is writing to Pam who is now at home with her parents in Wales waiting to hear where she will be posted next. He is hoping she will get a 'cushy job' in the Admiralty in London. This sets him off on another fantasy about how she must make sure she gets a helpful boss who will let her "leave the office at 11 for lunch and then not come back for the rest of the day". But reality soon crashes in

> *It's glorious to daydream about it, my darling but the cold facts are rather nasty. Since this LIAP scheme started only one of our officers has gone on leave. I had a month's leave a year ago after I escaped so if it is worked out on that basis I'll be a pensioner before I get my chance.*

LIAP stood for Leave in Advance of Python. Python was the original scheme for leave rotation that meant you had to serve for four years before guaranteeing leave. LIAP was more lenient and meant you could get leave after a couple of years overseas service as long as you had not had any previous leave. At this stage it seems a long shot as only a very few could make use of LIAP and the lucky ones were chosen by ballot. This mention of LIAP is the first of an on-going obsession with his chances of getting leave. For months he will live in hope of getting back to his girl only for those hopes to be dashed. The allocation of leave was a capricious process and for someone who was desperate to get home was a permanent anxiety.

However, things are further complicated when in the same letter he lets drop that there is a chance that the regiment may be sent to Burma.

> *It does sound like a life sentence now. I should be panting to go, but now it is the very last thing I can imagine being even further away from you.*
>
> *I dream of going home and being with you, but then some Jeremiah in the Mess who foretells frightful things like "Another go in Italy (which I so loathed) or a "short journey to Burma when you'll be lucky to see England in the next three years old man". At the very worst it can't be more than a year, but that's three hundred and sixty-five days without you*

I find it hard to believe that, all things being equal, he should be 'panting to go' to Burma. The Japanese were still in control and news of the fate of those captured in the Far East must have filtered through to those in the European theatre.

He ends with what must have been the heartfelt cry of so many at the fag-end of the war:

> *Pam, my dear darling, it cannot be forever. This beastly war must stop soon and we must be sent home soon and then there can't be any of this waiting for something that will never happen. It will happen God knows, but it's awfully hard waiting for it.*
>
> *Bless you sweetheart,*
>
> *All my love*
>
> *Drew.*

Two weeks later, and his yearning for her has not diminished with time:

> *It's been just seven weeks since I saw you or to be exact six weeks and seven days and darling it seems like seven life times. Unless something happens soon I'll be taking 'French Leave'. There's a plane that leaves Lydda Airport every day for home and they can't fill it.*

And he would indeed have to go Absent Without Leave

because the LIAP process is tortuous, the few allocations are drip fed out to the regiments. In the same letter he describes the LIAP draw. Thirty names in a hat. One of them has the word LEAVE on it. Everyone sits around in the Officers Mess and watches as each man's name is called and a slip is taken out:

> It never got round to me –'Leave' was shouted and the lucky man lowered the paper he had been reading, looked dazed and said "These things don't happen to me!". Oh, darling I am not whining but why couldn't it have been me. It would have been fate's reasonable reply to her last effort.

I assume he is referring to the weather stopping him getting to Cairo before she sailed back to England.

The regiment has moved into the desert to Dmier in Syria for more gunnery training. Both living conditions and the climate have deteriorated:

> *April 16th 1945*
>
> We are living in tents. It is sweltering hot all day then in the evening we sit in our coats and shiver. And the dust! Like Anzio, clouds of grey choking stuff that covers everything and you never feel clean. But on a clear day I can see the snow: our snow, my darling. I have been promised a weekend skiing, but I am almost afraid to go because it will be "last time" all

the time and it will be awfully lonely.

In the same letter he is anticipating VE day (Victory in Europe) which won't come for another three weeks, but they are without radio and news is trickling into their camp.

> *The news comes in every forty-eight hours but when it does it is so detached and impersonal but when the day (VE) is announced I can't see a lot of terrific parties taking place or if they do it will not be with any enthusiasm as far as I am concerned it will just be 'Thank God': it's such a beastly occupation war and all one really wants is to get the job finished and get home. Back to something one knows and for me my darling that is back to you. In some ways it will be like a string breaking, one has spent all one's time aiming at greater heights of training and efficiency, in fact the ability to kill, and then it suddenly loses all importance.*

I am not sure whether it was the living conditions but he has adopted a policy of self-restraint:

> *Darling, the joke of the moment is that I have gone "on the wagon" for a month. I don't really know why. About a week ago I decided I was hitting the bottle too hard and that it was not doing me a lot of good. I stopped dead and am still being virtuous. But I must say although I don't find it at all difficult, it is nice to have the odd 'corpse reviver' and the pre-meal gin is*

a pleasant habit and the after dinner Kümmel which makes me think of you.

Two days later he has his mind on more intimate matters.

26th April 1945

Darling an embarrassing question. What are your measurements? I believe the basics according to the Vogue advertisement are best. Bust, waist, hips. There are some lovely things one can get here. But the what-have-yous "the panties, scanties and huggie-snuggies" which they produced for my embarrassed inspection (the other man had no shame at all and gave some pretty lurid comments, but he had been married five years!). The most incredible remark, forgive me, was about a night dress and on being told the price, which was fantastic, he said "What all that for something to lay over the end of the bed". This is awful. Telling naughty stories or near naughty.

I am touched by his naïve sense of the 'naughty'. He recognises that he is no man of the world and his shameless friend can be excused on the grounds that he has been married for five years. Clearly no stranger to the joys of the bedroom. I cannot, of course, stop myself guessing about whether or not my mother and father actually slept together during their very brief encounter in the mountains. Reading this with its gauche presumption that somehow his Pam would disapprove, leads me to the conclusion that they probably got no further than passionate kissing in the airport at Lydda. An intimacy it has to be said that left him with a powerful memory of the scent of her hair.

He finishes the letter with yet more yearning, and he channels what a few years later with the publication of *Catch 22* would be called his inner Yossarian, who was trying get home from the war in Italy by claiming to be mad.

> *But darling mine, it can't and won't last, something is bound to happen. I know I have said it before, it is a sort of litany. I have to believe it otherwise I would go right off the rails, of course that would be the final irony of fate- if one went mad one would be sent home at once! I am sure you'd hate it sweetheart if I arrived home thinking I was an alarm clock.*

A week later on the 5th May, he is aware that the war is ending, (VE Day is just two days away) and he knows that his brother Tony has finally been released and must be on his way home. Tony was a survivor of The Great Escape:

> *My brother Tony ought to be arriving home any day now from Germany poor lad. It's a devil of a bump to go from the life of a fighter pilot to prisoner of war as suddenly as he did and he has done two and a half years – five months drove me desperate – and I imagine the boy has gone through the hoop a bit as he was in that awful shooting episode at Stalag Luft III when 47 were shot. He escaped that time and was recaptured. I gather he had a pretty rough deal*

> *afterwards and these last three months have been hell as they moved them around from camp to camp and we had no news. When he arrives back could you bear to see him. He'll probably be changed a lot from when I last saw him almost certainly he will be what you described as the 'brutal and licentious soldiers after they come out of action'. Do you remember over dinner at Mon Repos telling me what we were like coming out of action– sex starved was the description! I wasn't as bad as that was I darling?*

That dinner at Mon Repos took place just a few weeks after my father had indeed come out of action: nine months from Anzio to Monte Grande (which as he has told us in a previous letter he 'so loathed'). Pam seems familiar with these sex-starved young men, but it looks as if Drew was more restrained in his desires. His brother, on the other hand, did have a reputation as a lothario and I am assuming that he was giving her due warning that he might well try it on.

Now the letters keep coming: four or five a week. Much of it is mundane. He fills pages and pages with descriptions of regimental life with not a lot to do except once in a while to head off into the desert and fire off those twenty-five--pounder guns by way of practice and demonstrations for the top brass. He eats and drinks (a lot) in the officer's mess and there is reference to his fellow officers who are all equally preoccupied with thoughts of love and home. Each letter is full of longing: for an end to the war, for leave that will get him home and for the love of his short life. The extracts tell their own story.

May 8th 1945 VE Day

Pam my dear darling,

It's the day after VE day -and a complete anti-climax as I thought, it was beyond realisation that something must happen soon to finish this completely unbearable situation and separation. I got your letter the day before, when we knew that the war was over and quite honestly, such is the importance of these things, your letter was better for the morale than the news.

What was London like darling? We heard Churchill in the afternoon and the King in the evening. It sounded tremendous as if London had gone delirious from cheering and general noise. Darling mine, I would have pawned my immortal soul to have been there, then, with you. Here the King's speech came at ten o'clock at night. They had it on loudspeakers. I left the mess and listened to it in the open thinking that you would be listening at the same time.

16th May 1945

The two big events of today are that my brother Tony has arrived back safely in England. Thank God. At very long last. A telegram arrived this morning.
The other thing is that if I wait here for another three months, I'll almost certainly get command of the battery and be a Major. Sounds terrific doesn't it. And

there is also the 'feeler' that we might all go home together.

He is preoccupied by the regimental rumour mill, producing what he calls 'feelers'. These shards of information invariably raise his hopes only for them to be quickly dashed by subsequent more reliable sources.

Back in London, a few weeks after Pam's training is complete, she gets her posting. It is to the Admiralty, just off Horse Guards parade..

21st May 1945

It is marvellous that the London job has arrived. It does make all the difference to think of you there. Some dear admiral has done his job at last, but darling I can't see our chance to be together quite yet, although it does look as if our luck is beginning to turn. God knows it needs to.

Three months tomorrow since `I saw you last!

10th June 1945

There is such a bitter sweetness about being in love – darling mine – I have never had the courage to say it before. It does look so cold and lifeless on paper and to write it requires that cold blooded passion or rather the dispassionate condition with which one watches one's own shells killing other humans,

13th June 1945

It is one of those nights that are made for memories – just warm, the softest of breezes off the sea and a moon that leaves a track across the sea that looks as if it leads to you, from the purely navigational point it does, but to my somewhat love struck eye it includes an invitation to walk up the broad silver way and that you are at the end of it.

20th June 1945

This evening's peace was spoilt by some poor devil of a gunner coming around to see me with a letter from home. Oh, darling mine, it was pitiful. His wife was having a baby by another man. Obviously, we'll get him home on compassionate leave but that is no consolation to tell a man that's almost in tears and very much in love with his wife – she's obviously very young and insane with worry it looked like it from the letter. It left me feeling rather inadequate and helpless.

24th June 1945

I do remember Lydda Airport, the gate, you'll probably never forget it., but nor will I. You waited so long, –

the sight of your figure in the headlights and then you saying "Drew"- it's not an attractive word but Pam dear heart it's one of the many things I want to hear you say, it sounded so full of you.

27th June 1945

A letter from you, Pam my sweet, it was the letter I have wanted more than all the rest put together. I have known for ages that I loved you. There is no other frame of mind that would account for the condition that you have reduced me to and I am ashamed to say that I have never had the courage to say so. It does need guts (to put it crudely) to say "I love you". With writing it I feel as if it should come as a conclusion of some masterpiece of prose and not as the stuttering and ill written beginning of a letter. It's one of the occasions I wish I wasn't a common or garden soldier, but a long-haired poet with the gift of tongues.

19th July 1945

I am commanding the battery at the moment, Raymond is on leave, so drunk with the power I wield, life is fairly pleasant except for one major blot, the wettest fish you never met drew the last LIAP: the odds were 29 to 1 and he of all people got it. He doesn't really want it. He has no good reason for going home!

Pam, my dear heart, why can't I have more than the memories of one night when I had you to myself with no one else to disturb the feeling of knowing that you and I were together. I know I have a lot to be grateful that you did miss that plane at Lydda. Thank God.

22nd July 1945

Teddy's wife has sent him a copy of "Forever Amber"[22] which we are awaiting eagerly. I gather it's some thousand pages of pure sex as she put it: "I couldn't read much more after half a dozen chapters of solid sex and a woman who wasn't satisfied with her twelve men when I haven't even got my one!". It sounds like we have got to the verge of sex starvation, but we have heard so much about it that it must have something. What is your opinion of it?

Darling mine, if I wasn't so much in love with you, I'd write so much more sensible letters.

14th August 1945

Lots to say. First, it is so important to say that I love you Secondly, start crossing off the days with a

---

22. Forever Amber, which had sold 3m copies after its publication in 1944, and went on to become a bestseller in 16 countries was Kathleen Winsor's story of an English adventuress who becomes one of the mistresses of Charles II. It had been banned in Boston as "obscene and offensive". In banning the book, the Massachusetts attorney general had listed 70 references to sexual intercourse, 39 illegitimate pregnancies, seven abortions, 10 descriptions of women undressing in front of men, and 49 "miscellaneous objectionable passages".

> *four-month target from the day you get this letter, although it <u>may</u> be even better than that, but don't dream of it. It sounds like ages but it is something definite at last, at such long last too, darling. And finally, my promotion has come at last: I am now a major. I am drunk with pride.*
>
> *Pam my love everything good seems to be coming our way now: the end of the war (as far as we are concerned), my promotion and news of going back to you. something that is real at last.*

With the war finally over, the process of demobilising the fighting force began in earnest. More and more experienced soldiers were sent back to England and regiments disbanded. Those that were to remain as part of the standing army were reinforced with inexperienced recruits who knew nothing of war. It was frustrating for those who had become used to the comradeship built up over four years of combat.

20th August 1945

> *The next months are going to be so very difficult, all the demobilisation schemes and the whole Battery leaving very nearly so that all the men one knows disappear and the show has to be started again. It's depressing. On VE Day we were a first-rate Battery with a lot of experience and now we are losing the old, senior NCOs. And mere children are having to be*

promoted (myself for one, I am much too young for the job)

16th September 1945

I have at long last read 'Forever Amber' – an attempt by some female to pander to the public lust – she succeeds too. I think it's a shocking book, not that any of the scenes are pornographic but obviously she has tried hard and has managed to avoid the censors quite easily., as she merely catalogues the amorous adventures of an 'enthusiastic amateur' without any attempt to describe the adventure itself!

8th November 1945

The big tragedy has occurred, the faithful Hughes has gone on release. I did hate seeing him go, he has been there for so long I am now really appreciating how much he did do. He is going to be a sorter at the `GPO in Merthyr Tydfil.

The 'faithful Hughes' was my father's 'batman'. In the British army every commissioned officer would have been assigned a batman although in the Second World War these servant soldiers would have been shared. Hughes would have looked after my father: running messages, setting up his accommodation and acting as a valet. Today it feels very old fashioned and a reflection of the patrician ethos of the army. I like to think that my father was a sympathetic master. I was reassured by the evidence I found in a letter written by Billy Hughes' parents to Drew's mother. It is dated May 1943 a few weeks after my father had been captured at Recce Ridge.

59 Ernest Street,
Merthyr Tydfil

Dear Mrs Bethell,

We received a letter from our boy (Gunner W.G. Hughes) today and both my husband and myself are more than sorry to learn that Captain Bethell is a prisoner of war, and I know by Billy's letter that he feels it very keenly. He could never speak too highly of your son and I can assure you it was a great comfort to us that he had not only a good officer but a very good friend.

15th November 1945

Weather has been perfect until today when the wind started: God what a wind. The tents nearly take off every gust, and it is purely a question of time before mine goes. There is dust everywhere which sticks to the sweat: very horrid.

December 3rd 1945

This last week. I was commanding the Regiment because everyone else was away. I had my three days, drunk with power. I harried them until I achieved something of the standard of march discipline that they ought to have acquired after six years of war. Darling, mine, you know you are in love with a soldier, it is a magnificent job, but it is going to be awfully boring listening to one because one has become so accustomed to endless shop.

By the next time he writes it seems that all hopes of getting back by Christmas are dashed. He is miserable and angry.

10th December 1945

Pam, sweetheart mine,

I am afraid this is a letter, not the letter and it is no joy to write. I will not be spending Christmas with you. The leave is very definitely off, not a snowball's chance in hell of it coming this month and worst still not even January as far as I can see it. Sweetheart I have, sworn, blinded, and cursed and lost my temper. When I was told that I wouldn't see you this year, it was a life sentence. That is because I am so in love with you.

Then a couple of days later, once again, his hopes are raised.

14th December 1945

The leave question got a big fillip this afternoon when the Colonel told me that there is a scheme a foot to send regular officers home for 28 days – independently of LIAP and that he is pressing to fly us home – oh my darling it is another ' feeler' and I am so tired of these 'maybes' all the time, but he did seem quite serious about it although I am so very cynical now and bolshie too. It's hard not to be.

Darling, I dare not say anything about leave, I feel if I do it will not come off. Rather like that childish game I used to play with myself at Christmas time "If I say out loud that I want a bicycle it won't come" so I torture myself by not saying a word about it.

Talking of Christmas, I haven't sent you a Christmas present because I was assuming that I would be bringing it you in person. It will have to be a 'leave present'.

27th December 1945

No mail for days now. No one had any letters over Christmas at all.

It's such an unnatural festival Christmas in the army, there's only one way to spend it and that's at home. That's with you darling.

But this is the big news. They are going to add an extra 28 days Regular Officers 'end of war' leave, so it will be two whole delirious months! That is something to talk about. At the moment my name is at GHQ being approved for leave in January. I should fly and that means, my darling, with you by the 28 or 30th at worst. I am so very frightened we might be disappointed again that I hardly dare walk into the Adjutant's office to hear the worst.

29th December 1945

Sunday is such a magnificent day, the long lie in, the idle dressing, walking to and fro dressed in next to nothing, putting in a new blade in the razor, washing, straightening up your photographs, smoking the first cigarette for the day (it's awful the amount I get through now it is so much desk work that does it)

British soldiers were given free cigarettes throughout the war. Tobacco was considered essential for morale and Players and Woodbines were included in ration packs. My father went on to smoke through most of the rest of his life and particularly heavily when he was on a desk job. I fear this probably contributed to his heart attack at a relatively early age.

Finally, a few days later it comes. The news he has been waiting for after hopes raised and then cruelly dashed. No more talk of flying back in a few hours, but rather a week-long journey by ship, train and eventually ferry to England.

5th January 1946

News! I am to go on leave on the 18th in thirteen days' time. I say it with a combination of triumph and fear just in case a large spanner is thrown into the works <u>again</u>. Until I am actually on the ship I am not going to believe it's true. If it is, I ought to be home on the 28th and then, darling, we can go mad. I don't think I will fly, it's almost certainly ship and train across France.

I think I have told you before that I am rather frightened, in some ways of meeting you again, dear heart. One thing is I clear I will be so damned dumb in the presence of a cool young woman, with whom I know I am in love- darling do you feel the same?

16th January 1946

The last letter before I start home! Darling it will be almost a year exactly since I met you, in some ways it's yesterday: the dinner at Maisie's - it's still so fresh – something that hasn't happened to me before. Then there are the endless days of waiting, the expectation of seeing you in Cairo. Then the letters. So many letters. Then the disappointments of leave being put off.

On the 19th of January he is leading a group of sixty men all off on leave. They get on a train that immediately gets derailed, is put back on the track and they pick up more men "*all wearing grins as big as the proverbial cat that swallowed the canary. It is a glorious feeling darling to know that we have actually started on the way. I'll be seeing you in fourteen days"* They arrive in Port Said and wait for a ship. They wait for two days. Then they are taken across the harbour to an Italian ship that should take them home.

> *Only to find that the Italian crew had mutinied, wanting to be paid in sterling and not in lira. So, all of us, some sixty officers and 700 men had to come back across the harbour to our base. We were all a bit down in the mouth with some uttering horrid threats as to what they would do if they had half a chance with the Italian crew. We'll have to wait for another ship but whatever happens I'll still get 28 days leave.*
>
> *23rd January 1946*
>
> *We may start today, but up to 10 am and nothing has appeared yet.*

But it seems that something did happen later in the day because he does leave Port Said on that Italian ship. It took three days on board to get to Toulon where they transferred to a troop train that took another three days to make its way up to Dieppe. I feel sure he would have tried to ring Pam and warn her that he was due in London the next day. He crossed the Channel on the 30th of January 1945. Another troop train would have taken him up to London where I like to think he would have met my mother. But, I suspect it might have been his mother who got there first.

Stoke Newington, London November 2024

Dear Dad,

I do hope you are not embarrassed by those letters. I think they are a remarkable account of a love affair nurtured through absence. I have to confess that I never saw the raw passionate side of you that you reveal about yourself, and yet you are so recognisable. The energy and enthusiasm mixed with your gregarious engagement with the men you both worked with and played with, these are all traits I recognise. And you were humane, you could empathise with the man whose wife is having a baby with another and I know that you often displayed that same humanity throughout your life. Equally that passion and enthusiasm could just as easily be transformed into intolerance and bad temper. I remember that as well. I also recognise your inhibited expectations of yourself and of others. You were a product of your up-bringing: whenever you were faced with adversity or contradiction you reverted to a formulaic response governed by the expectations of the time.

And then there were those flashes of innocence and naiveté, whether it was buying underwear or reading what passed as pornography: you sounded your age. And it was this almost guileless side of you that shaped my prurient conjecture as to whether or not you had slept with Pam during that ridiculously short dalliance that led to such a powerful infatuation. You repeatedly write about how the trip down to Haifa was remarkable because you were alone for the first time (although there was the walk back from Mon Repos, presumably just the two of you). If that was true, and that up until then you were in the company of friends, I cannot stop myself speculating as to what happened over that evening when you were finally alone in what you describe as "that beastly place". You were clearly falling in love, but it is still hard to understand quite how you generated such an intense longing for each other. Surely it must have been fuelled by an intimate physical connection. It must have been more than a snog to ignite that avalanche of letters.

I have left you finally embarking on the elusive and much yearned for passage back to England and your lover. Up until the last, each moment of optimism seems to have been shattered by frustrating delay. It seemed to be a lottery with you drawing the short straw. Eventually your luck changed and you were on your way.

However, before I try to work out how you get on and whether the reality lived up to the expectation, I need to break off the chronology to address what we would nowadays call 'the elephant in the room'. 1st Division was posted to Palestine to train and re-group. You were there to recover and eventually start the process of demobilising the wartime troops and re-building with younger, greener men. However, as the months went by your presence in what was then called British Palestine Mandate coincided with the escalating Jewish resistance to British rule and policies around the immigration of survivors of the war in Europe. Your letters were still being censored so it is understandable that you were very circumspect and I want to think that the almost light-hearted tone you adopted when referring to your involvement in the Internal Security activities was intended to allay Pam's worst fears.

However, when looked at from my perspective in 2024 with the ongoing devastation of the region and the ruthless retaliation of the Zionist government of Israel against the Palestinian people, it has a much darker resonance. For that reason, I need to look behind your brief and oblique references to 'the bother' to try and establish what you and your men were actually doing. The term 'Internal Security' has an ominous ring but I have no right to hold you to account. You were doing your job. The war records of the Parachute Regiment which was doing the same work put it best: "Of all the burdens cast on British soldiers by politicians, Palestine was one of the heaviest". And I would add, 'least reported'. I have had to do a lot of digging.

With love,

Hum

CHAPTER 20

The Palestine Question

British Palestine. May 1945 to December 1946.

I still have my father's medals and they include one with a stylish purple and green ribbon which has a bar inscribed with the word 'Palestine 1945-48'. It nestles between his Italy Star and his Africa Star. I have referred to how the Italian campaign was under-reported in the annals of the Second World War. But the Palestine campaign has been virtually ignored. And yet over a three-year period seven hundred and fifty British service personnel were killed. Reading my father's letters, I can see that it was rarely as gruelling as the battle for Italy and yet if I read between the lines, there were times when the regiment's work was sometimes almost as intense and frightening.

The struggle in Palestine has a long history that predates the Balfour Declaration which in 1917 announced the establishment of "a national home for the Jewish people". However, the conflict that blew up in 1945-46 has its roots in the Holocaust. During the Second World War the British restricted the entry into Palestine of European Jews escaping Nazi persecution. They had imposed a limit on Jewish immigration in the summer of 1939, anxious to end the disturbances in Palestine and to secure the support of the Egyptians and oil-rich Saudis ahead of the looming conflict in Europe. By 1945 this policy had provoked armed Jewish resistance. Initially there were three groups ranging from the moderate to the avowed terrorist group known as the Stern Gang. By the middle of 1945 the three groups had combined uniting those who looked to Britain for help in establishing their national homeland and those who wished to use terrorism to drive the British out. The combined group was called the Haganah.

The first mention of 'bother' comes in a letter dated 25th May 1945.

> *There doesn't seem any chance of leave on the present form. You have probably heard of the bother on the wireless and unless a miracle happens I imagine we will get involved eventually.*

I have had difficulty finding what news might have found its way onto the wireless at this early stage of the conflict. The Stern Gang were conducting raids on police stations and some transport hubs. There was a report of sabotage of an oil refinery owned by the Iraq Petroleum Company and the suggestion that this might affect oil supplies to the Far East campaign. However, he would not have mentioned it unless there was a growing sense that his regiment would soon be involved

The next time he refers to the situation is when he writes about the election result. This was the election that brought in Clement Attlee's Labour government. It occurred on the 31st May 1945 but it takes him almost two months before he comments on it. I am not surprised that my father disapproved of a socialist government, although I am confused that his main complaint lay in his fear that their foreign policy would be no match for Stalin. However, it is the attitude of the new Labour government to the Palestine Question that did surprise me:

28th July 1945

This election result has surprised most people immensely, I think they approve, but God knows, I don't. It's impossible to imagine what the form is with C. Atlee competing with Joe Stalin, I am afraid I just can't see it happening, not with any success for us anyhow and the other thing is the Labour boys' views on the Jews and Palestine: that's going to cause no mean spot of bother here in the next eighteen months. Please God I am out before it starts.

It seems that in stark contrast to the views held by the party today, influential figures in the Labour movement, including Nye Bevan and Michael Foot, had brought a distinctly pro-Zionist influence to bear on Labour's Palestine policy. It is easy to forget that in the early years the Israeli state was informed by a socialist ideology that was reflected in the Kibbutz movement. It was this aspect of Zionism that caused Michael Foot to inform the House of Commons in July 1946: "If I were a Jew and lived in

Palestine, I should certainly be a member of the Haganah." And as for my father's hope that he would be 'out before it starts", it was yet another example of wishful thinking.

Two months passed before the situation becomes serious enough for Drew to refer to it in a letter. Once again, he is doing his best to reassure.

> 20th October 1945
>
> *One thing while I remember – should you read that things are happening here. Don't worry dear heart, it is always made out to be so much worse than it really is. The papers have to find something to report, to pander to a public that is used to large scale murder (sic) so a report has to be lurid if it is to be good, and besides nothing can happen to me because we are owed so much in the way of luck. Eight months darling missing each other and most of it not knowing how long it will last.*

In fact, within days, his regiment changed from training to active service:

> *Regimental records:*
> *23rd to 31st October 1945:*
>
> *Regiment put onto IS (Internal Security) role and full duties*

Anti-mortar and railway patrols carried out daily. Roadblocks and armed patrols nightly.

On the 26th October he is aware that trouble is brewing although he is sanguine about how the British troops will respond:

For the last few days the feeling has been rather like sitting on the safety valve of a very large boiler that is going to explode anyhow. I don't think there will be trouble, we have got so many soldiers and so much assorted ironmongery that any insurrection would be slapped down so quickly that it just wouldn't pay.

However, on October 31st the situation escalated with numerous incidents up and down the territory. The attacks included bombings on police vehicles, railway sites, and the Haifa oil refinery. The regiment was based at Al Tira twenty-five miles north of Tel Aviv and in the epicentre of much of the trouble. Drew was suddenly back in combat conditions.

8th November 1945

Work is getting harder and harder, more and more playing around at night and although nothing has happened of importance, it is going to be a relief when the balloon goes up and the proper fighting starts. That it is going to happen is more or less certain.

It seems that there were no casualties during this phase,

although there must have been a lot of tension around those patrols and road blocks.

15th November 1945

No chance to answer your letters until today. The same everlasting story of flap after flap which means unnecessary hours out of bed and feeling so tired. Yesterday I sent out five patrols leading one myself.

Then he writes about protests in Tel Aviv:

18th November 1945

Please God the war here seems to have died down except for the little effort in Tel Aviv which was useful as it allowed some of that surplus energy to expend itself and for a change it cost us nothing except some bruises and it did show the Yehedi that we are standing no damn nonsense. As a result, we can take the days more easily but night is still hours of patrols, road blocks and watching and waiting for something to happen.

I am not sure in what way the "war" had died down. The night time patrols could still be fraught. The Haganah resistance was still at its height fuelled by the British government's continued refusal to allow in more refugees from Europe. At about this time the Anglo-American Committee of Enquiry on Palestine was established to resolve the question of whether a further

100,000 Jews would be allowed into the territory. As yet no resolution was forthcoming and the attacks on the British presence continued.

So, what was the 'little effort' in Tel Aviv that required British troops? The matter came up in parliament:

HANSARD 16 November 1945 vol 415

Hansard November 18th

The Under-Secretary of State for the Colonies (Mr. Creech Jones)

On the evening of the 14th November, rioting occurred in Tel Aviv, following mass meetings by Jews in protestation against the Government statement of policy (not to allow in the 100,000). Damage was extensive. An attack on the Post Office was frustrated by police and military action. As six baton charges were insufficient to disperse the crowd, soldiers who had been brought up to reinforce the police fired ten rounds. The crowd withdrew. Other crowds stoned the police and soldiers. After verbal warning and after three soldiers had been injured, four rounds were fired with the desired effect.

I can only assume that the Gunners of 19th Field Regiment took part in those baton charges which allowed them to 'expend their surplus energy'. They may even have fired those warning shots. It may have cost them nothing but a few bruises but the protests were widespread and the repercussions upon the residents of Tel Aviv are clearly described in this anonymous letter published in the Jerusalem Post and yet addressed in English to the British forces:

> *I am writing you as a plain citizen of Tel-Aviv to tell you what most of us feel in these days of heartbreak and bitterness. You have been in occupation of our city for nearly a week. Your tanks are rolling through our streets, your aeroplanes have been droning on our roofs, your rockets have been lighting up our skies. It has been a nice little nerve war against the peaceful citizens of a modern city.*
>
> *Do you think you have frightened us? There is among the 200,000 Jews of Tel-Aviv not a single family which has not lost some relative in Hitler's death camps and gas chambers. Do you think that people who have gone through these agonies are going to be frightened by the sight of tanks or the glare of rockets?*
>
> *I am sure a good many of you hate the whole ugly business. You are not hired soldiers. You are the free citizens of a free country who joined up to fight the worst tyranny on earth. You have done your job and you have done it gallantly. You are now being employed on a very different kind of job. You have been sent to this country, so you have been told, "to*

fight the Jews", in other words, to break the resistance of a desperate people against a most horrible betrayal.

My father's flippancy in his letter to Pam seems crass in contrast to this humane entreaty. Although I fear he accurately reflects the attitudes of his men after an action that at least got the adrenalin flowing. I certainly do not feel in a position to judge him at this distance. Nevertheless, I would like to feel that, had he read that letter with its reasonable appeal to a better nature, he would have paused for a moment to consider the impact of the engagement.

And just a few days later he writes about another flare-up of resistance from what he calls 'the enemy'

25th November 1945

Last night the enemy was naughty again, a night of alarms and excursions, although as far as we were concerned no damage done – someone else had a spot of nonsense you'll have heard it before we did on the wireless.

According to newspaper reports the attacks took place close to the 19th Regiment camp at Al Tira:

> Palestine was relatively quiet until November 25, when the Irgun attacked British police stations at Hadera and near Herzliya (*10 miles from Al Tira*) which were used as watch points to detect

illegal Jewish immigration, using automatic fire and explosives. Six British and eight Arab policemen were wounded. British troops and police subsequently carried out search operations on November 25 and November 26 against the Jewish settlements looking for insurgents and arms. They met violent resistance from Jewish civilians in the settlements as well as large numbers of Jews from outside who raced to confront the British, and clashes broke out which resulted in 8 Jews killed and 75 wounded.

I find myself conflicted in reading and researching about this period. Eighty years have passed and the Israeli state is now dominant in the region and currently engaged in its own defence using often unacceptable levels of force and brutality. The Palestinian Arabs are under constant threat of displacement with next to no hope of a secure state of their own. Whilst in Gaza the threat has turned into an horrific reality with the devastating demolition of the place and its people. It is essential to avoid conflating anti-Zionist sentiment with anti-Semitism, and yet I cannot help myself in condoning my father in his antagonism towards the Zionist terrorists. The violent tactics of the Irgun seem to be a foretaste of what the extreme Zionist leaders have employed in more recent times. Indeed, there were plenty of examples of Jewish settlers ruthlessly taking over land from Palestinian Arabs in the 1940s, activity which takes place now on a grand scale with violence and impunity. At the same time, the recalcitrance of the British Government in not allowing more immigrants to enter the territory in 1945 puts me in mind of similar reactionary impulses that prompted all the other struggles to resist colonial repression. I have to accept that my father was a participant in a similar imposition by a British government that believed it had the right to determine the fate of distant lands.

Eight months pass before he mentions the troubles again. In the meantime, he has been on leave and proposed to my mother. There is no mention of road blocks or patrols and the Regiment seems to be back in training mode. His letters are full of yearning and making plans for Pam to join him after they are married. He feels that as the conflict escalates again, it will be over before she arrives. But then in June reality intrudes. They are back in action.

> 20th June 1946
>
> *It is hard to realise how serious it is, but obviously it must be as all the brass hats are rather worried. I think it will be good if a real war starts because then we can hit and hit hard. Nowadays, we, the Army have to stand back and let ourselves be hit, except yesterday when a Yehedi tried rushing a road block and was shot, most unusual and most gratifying although its rather inhumane to say so. It's got to the state that as I write my revolver lanyard is looped around my wrist. It sounds most dramatic but everyone has to sleep with his weapon tied to him.*

His use of the term 'Yehedi' is confusing. It is not widely used in reports at the time, but it is clearly the way he and his fellow soldiers refer to the Jewish activists. I am disturbed by his use of the word "gratifying" although I can have some sympathy with his frustration at having to "stand back and let ourselves be hit". British soldiers were killed quite regularly during this period and mostly not in combat but rather when isolated or vulnerable. He has his pistol close at hand because there were too many examples of Jewish fighters getting into the British camps.

A month later the defining act of terrorism occurred in Jerusalem.

22nd July 1946

I gather the King David Hotel in Jerusalem has been blown up and fifty people killed. Bob Harris and I were in Jerusalem yesterday having a quick drink in the King David too! Just twenty-four hours before the bomb! A lucky escape.

Until then everything seemed to be a lot calmer, and now the troubles start again. Damn these Yehedis. The villagers in Benyamina and Pardess Hanna were so nice this evening too. I met with the Muchtars of both places to ask about whether they had horses that I could ride. Both are looking around for me and giving me an answer in a week's time, but this will obviously put the lid on that for some time to come – damn the Irgun and the Haganah and the rest.

In fact, the final death toll was ninety-one, many of whom were British. The atrocity came up in parliament.

HANSARD July 24th 1946

Mr. Eden
asked the Prime Minister whether he has any statement to make on the bomb outrage at the British Headquarters in Jerusalem.

The Prime Minister (Mr. Attlee)
Hon. Members will have learned with horror of the brutal and murderous crime committed yesterday in Jerusalem. Of all the outrages which have occurred in Palestine, and they have been many and horrible in the last few months, this is the worst. By this insane act of terrorism 93 innocent people have been killed or are missing in the ruins. The latest figures of casualties are 41 dead, 52 missing and 53 injured. Every effort is being made to identify and arrest the perpetrators of this outrage. The work of rescue in the debris, which was immediately organised, still continues. The next-of-kin of casualties are being notified by telegram as soon as accurate information is available. The House will wish to express their profound sympathy with the relatives of the killed and with those injured in this dastardly outrage.

Whilst there was condemnation of the attack by some of the Jewish community, there was controversy over the fact that the Irgun actually made three warning phone calls over twenty minutes before the bombs went off. Initially this was denied by the British but many years later it was accepted that the warnings had been received but were ignored. The Israeli paper *Haaretz* in a piece written on the 75th anniversary described the incident and refers to the continuing controversy.

> The Irgun, headed by Menachem Begin, tried to warn the British to evacuate the King David in advance. But nobody listened, and 91 people died.
>
> The act of terror shocked the British, and helped accelerate their decision to withdraw from Palestine two years later. It also led to a split within the Jewish community: the mainstream Jewish Agency and Haganah attempted to dissociate themselves from the operation - though it had in fact been carried out at their behest.
>
> To this day, Revisionists and Labor-Zionist sympathisers still argue about the propriety of the attack – and even whether it was an act of "terrorism" – as well as responsibility for the large toll in human life.

Two days after the bombing of the King David he writes about the retaliation:

24th July 1946

Trouble with a capital 'T', all Yehedi houses, cinemas, restaurants, in fact everything Yehedi has been put out of bounds and all speech with them has been to all intents and purposes forbidden.

He is referring to a letter issued to all officers by General Barker, the British commander of British Forces in Palestine, two days after the King David Hotel bombing, using phrases that have since become notorious. The letter demanded:

the non fraternisation with the Jewish community of Palestine and in so doing they shall suffer punishment and be made aware of the contempt and loathing with which we regard their conduct. We will be punishing them in a way the race dislikes as much as any: by striking at their pockets.

The order was only intended for senior officers but was leaked and widely circulated. The rabid antisemitism of these instructions was seen as 'an embarrassing blunder' which tarnished Britain's image and undermined any sympathy there may have been for the carnage at the St David's Hotel. It also reflected a failure to acknowledge the dark shadow of the Holocaust which gave a context to much of the resistance.

My father does not mention the 'troubles' in his letters for another three months. However, as we will see he has been distracted by his wedding and honeymoon. A couple of weeks after he returns to his regiment, he writes:

> November 17th 1946
>
> *The nonsense in Palestine is getting worse and I do think the crisis is coming, I gather that the government has said to all intents and purposes "right we'll do absolutely nothing until the Conference[23] and give the leaders the chance to call off the terrorists and if they don't we'll give them hell. I gather the hell raising will start sometime next month. At the moment it is pure murder and nothing else and is aimed at eliminating British soldiers. The hammer must come down soon and when it does I think that Palestine will resemble Germany. The Jews will be treated like a conquered people. They won't like it.*

This is the last time he mentions the Palestinian question because he is just six weeks away from his permanent departure from the Middle East. Although the situation continued to defy easy solutions, violence continued until a resolution of sorts was proposed in November 1947 with the UN plan for a Partition and two separate states for Palestinians and Jews. It did not quell the violence and was a followed by another year of Civil War. I am pleased my father got out when he did.

[23.] The **London Conference of 1946–1947**, which took place between September 1946 and February 1947, was called by the British Government of Clement Attlee to resolve the future governance of Palestine and negotiate an end of the Mandate. The Conference's failure to reach agreements between Arabs and Jews regarding the future of Palestine led Britain to renounce the Mandate and "submit the problem to the judgment of the United Nations."[2]

CHAPTER 21
Proposal, Marriage and Me

UK and Palestine. February 1946 to December 1946.

Before exploring the Palestine question, we left Drew on the verge of arriving back home for what turned out to be two months leave. It is a make-or-break moment for this relationship which he has managed to sustain over eleven months merely by a steady stream of correspondence. The last time he set eyes on Pam was in Lydda RAF Base, more than a year ago, when they spent an evening together due to her cancelled flight. But it was only one evening alone, in what he describes as that "beastly place". It was not even a night of passion. And yet it was enough for him to pour his heart out in over fifty letters all of which assume that the fragile and short-lived encounter on the Lebanon slopes would be enough on which to build and sustain an intense relationship. The big question must have been: is this relationship for real? Will the physical reality live up to the fantasy world they have created via the written word, when they finally do meet again in the flesh? In a letter written a few days before he departs for England he expresses some of that trepidation:

> *It's so hard to explain what I want when we do meet. The very nearness of you makes me rather frightened of myself. That I'll see you so soon that all the things I have been saving up for you – the words "I love you" written so many times now – embraces everything – darling mine I fear I'll make a fool of myself. I have a funny feeling in my chest even writing this. God knows what it is going to be like when I do see you.*

However, it will not be quite as simple as them rushing into each other's arms on the station platform. He has another woman in his life who will be making her own demands. Back in November he is already concerned about this split loyalty:

> *As for leave, to revert to planning, the first person I want to see when I get home is you my love. I do want you so much. I admit that first I must go and see my mother, poor dear, she has had rather a tough war with Tony and I away for so long, but darling it is a two way pull all the time and I know so well which way I want to go.*

I have very little to go on when it comes to working out what happens once he sets foot on home soil. He will spend much of his two months leave with Pam and will meet her parents, but he must also honour his obligations to his own mother. He writes just two letters in that period: slim pickings for the enquiring son. However, together they give a potent picture of both the joys and the tribulations of his pursuit of this woman.

The first letter makes it clear that when they eventually did meet for real, the passion had not dissipated over the twelve months and it looks very much as if they have slept together because he proposes to her on the stairs of a hotel.

2nd March 1946

> *I don't mind anything now that it is certain. It was the uncertainty before I came on leave. I knew that I loved you, darling mine but until I had seen you and you had said 'yes' it was rather difficult. I think we should subscribe to a small memorial plaque put up on the stairs at the McIntyre Hotel. 'Here was it that Drew proposed to Pam. And she accepted his proposal'.*

I am delighted that the proposal was a success. My very existence depended on a positive response. He has been in the country for a month by the time he writes that letter so it is hard to ascertain how quickly he got around to proposing. However, he will have definitely spent time with his own mother as well as with Pam's parents. Later in the same letter he suggests that he has yet to tell his mother that he is engaged, but is receiving advice from his future mother-in-law:

> *Your mother has said that I was not to rush my mama – a difficult operation-she knows most of the form but I can see that it is going to require a lot of tact!*

"A lot of tact" would appear to be an understatement. Two

days later he is writing to his fiancé from his mother's house. It is not going well:

> 4th March 1946
>
> Pam sweetheart mine,
>
> The phone call this evening was quite useless, the trouble was that the whole household can hear every word that one says on that damned telephone, and I still have some embarrassment in telling the world that I love you – at least letting them hear me say so.
>
> Mummy is peeved that I hadn't told her everything, not that I blame her. I am certain I gave the wrong impression about my mama but you know her, not as well as you should, as she didn't know, when you were here, that I had asked you to marry me nor that you sweetheart mine had made me so very happy when you said that you would. But next time you come down it will be very much better, darling it has been my fault all along if I hadn't been a damned fool and had told her from the very start it wouldn't have happened. – forgive me.

I am able to empathise with my father. I have myself prevaricated when it came to sharing unwelcome news with my mother. I too have found it hard to brace myself for the inevitable emotional backlash. I have often reassured myself that it is better to postpone the discomfort until a more propitious time. And yet I also know that the situation rarely benefits from delay, indeed it usually makes matters worse: as my dear father discovers. At the same time, I know from my mother's later testimony that she found her mother-in-law very difficult. 'Mama', as she was known, gave my mother the strong impression that she was not 'good enough' for her boy.

It is easy to side with my mother against a hostile prospective mother-in-law. However, I have to acknowledge that, when I consider what she had been through, it is not surprising that she had mixed feelings about losing her son to matrimony. Just over ten years ago her husband had shot himself leaving her suddenly impoverished and devoid of the status that meant so much to her. She was also needing to care for her three sons. She had done her best and then the war came. Her eldest son was wounded on the beach at Dunkirk and then captured in North Africa, her second son was shot down and imprisoned and her youngest son was evacuated to Canada. She had to survive months of terrifying uncertainty as to the fate of her warrior sons. I cannot be too surprised that when she eventually does get her eldest son back into her home, she is upset to find that far from devoting his love and affection to her, he has adoring eyes for another woman. No wonder she is aggrieved and recalcitrant.

He finishes that letter with a schedule for his last month of leave in the spring of 1946:

March 8th Friday: *see you again*
March 18th and 19th London?   *Both mothers!*
April 6th: *Hell! I leave you.*

I have no account of how it went with that meeting of the mothers in London. I recall a similar first meeting of my parents with the parents of my wife. It too was in London and I recall a sticky encounter. In-laws do not always get on. I should imagine that the mood music was not very soothing, as my father's defensive and sceptical single parent met up with my mother's gregarious and affable parents who had been beguiled by Drew's charm. However, it requires less speculation to appreciate how he was feeling about the 'hell' of the departure on April 6th. The next letter comes from Toulon. He has crossed the Channel and taken the tedious train journey down through France to the southern port where he is waiting for a ship to take him back to Egypt. He is waiting to depart and his mind is on Pam and the time they spent together.

12th April 1946

I am so humbly grateful for the last two months. I hadn't realised it was possible to be so happy, and you darling mine made me so. It wasn't until I saw you leaning out of the carriage that I even started to realise what was happening – that you were going – oh darling. I felt for that first night as if I had lost you forever.

My only regret about the leave was that I wish I had not been so brutal about mama. If only I had realised how little she was asking and how much it hurt her not to get it since it did spoil some of the time, not between us, but between us and her. Thank God she finally caught onto the idea early on that I had found someone very wonderful. Darling you are wonderful. Everything that any man could want and every time I think of it the luckier I know myself to be.

The image of him watching her depart on a train brought back a similar scene in the film *Brief Encounters*. The anguish of separation on the station platform in Carnforth. I heard the strains of Rachmaninoff's Second Piano Concerto as I read.

By mid-April 1945 he is back with his regiment and once again I am faced with a stack of letters. As before, he is writing to his now fiancée at least four times a week: long letters in his tiny handwriting. Whilst he tells her about his life and work, there are three recurring and more pressing themes. First, his delight at the potential joys of marriage and his good fortune in loving and being loved by Pam. Second, there is a wedding to be arranged and there are regular references to the decisions that must be made. Finally, he is fixated on how she might come and join him in Palestine once they are married. Pre-war it was accepted that army wives would be accommodated close to their spouses. However, each of his letters have the initials O.A.S. on the envelope: On Active Service. It is less than a year since the war in Europe ended and although the military presence in Palestine is initially perceived as a warm haven to recover and train after the ordeals of the Italian campaign, the tensions around a Jewish homeland mean that there is great uncertainty over whether or not wives will be allowed to join their husbands.

21st of April 1946

If darling mine, mutual and unending love, carrying with it mutual trust and sympathy, endless understanding (and your mother says it does) go to make a happy marriage – then dearest heart, we will be such a very happy couple. I feel that with you behind me -rather beside me- there is nothing that as a family you and I cannot do and as a soldier nothing is beyond me.

Now the news. Married families are going to be allocated married quarters in August!! Oh darling, darling mine, it is going to be so wonderful to have you here. There is of course a snag: it is provided that Palestine doesn't burst into flames. Damn these Yehedis.

I do not have my mother's letters but it seems that she has brought up the question of whether to have children and when that should happen.

16th May

I do agree with you about children. Let's have a year without a nipper anyway. It will give us time to get to know each other although dearest heart we don't want to wait much longer than that. If you are going to have a family it is best to have them young – while the going is good and before one is positively senile

> *when they grow up. I must admit I loathe the little blighters when they howl, it carries so far, and seems to go right through one's head after ten minutes.*

She has also suggested where they might go for a honeymoon. There had been some thought of touring in France, but it seems my mother has a more adventurous suggestion.

> *Honeymoon, darling, the idea of Sweden is a v. good idea. Getting a car across there could prove difficult, although I don't think it is quite so essential there as it would be in France.*

A few days later and he brings up the question of what to wear.

> *20th May*
>
> *More planning - do you want me to wear uniform or a morning coat? I haven't got a morning coast for a start, although I have got to get one some time, so it is exactly as you want.*

In his next letter he is in the mood for more reminiscence. He is looking at those photos from the week they met on the slopes.

> *23rd May*
>
> *I was looking at photographs from Feb 12th last year. Darling, do you remember that dinner we had,*

> *of course you do, when we won the money from the fruit machine, and you were wearing that blue dress and your hair so shining swept back glistening from your dear face. That last part sticks in my memory. We talked of shipboard romances (?) and the number of engagements that didn't come off on the way from England to Egypt. I must admit I was petrified every time I thought of it afterwards – how we didn't approve of short engagements. And yet I know that if I had got to Cairo for that weekend before you left, I would have asked you to marry me, in despite what we said. But now I think, although we both hated the separation, it was so good for us.*

It is one of the many 'sliding doors' moments. Had the weather not prevented him from flying down to Cairo on the first weekend after they met, perhaps he would have proposed. I cannot help speculating how that might have changed the story. Would she have said 'yes' and then perhaps taken a lesson from all those failed shipboard romances? Could it have been a case of acting in haste and repenting at leisure? Or, is he right that their courtship actually did benefit from the prolonged separation?

It seems that the matter of parenthood was on both their minds. I think she must have raised the issue of whether it was possible to be a 'radiant mother'. It causes him to reveal his ambivalence about the whole business and argue for delay.

> *May 26th 1946*
>
> *"Radiant Motherhood" is very good, only darling our*

effort mustn't look like a shrivelled little monkey. I suppose all babies have to start like that, or can one produce a fairly polished edition? I fail to understand why all mothers should be radiant! Someone with a pretty warped sense of humour thought that one up. Anyhow precious we will try the' radiant mother' and 'fond father' act after we have seen what married life is like "we two" as opposed to "we three".

A day later and there are more mundane matters on his mind.

27th May 1946

Talking sordid finance. If I go on as I am now (i.e. remain a major for the next year or so) we ought not do too badly. We'll get my pay and marriage allowance £620 +£228 = £848 a year untaxed, much less of course taxed. But we do get extra allowances out here so with luck it should be around £750 a year. I think we'll be able to live quite comfortably on that. But if I go down to Captain we are going to be damned hard up.

As the war ended more and more men were demobbed and were replaced often by younger less experienced officers. It meant that my father who was battle experienced had been promoted to Major ahead of his time. He was right to fear a demotion once the army settled back into its peace time complement. He is coming down from the euphoria of his engagement. He is seeking certainty when there is little to be had.

31st May 1946

Sweetheart, I have been rather depressed, but I am certain that if we go ahead and get married then the most important thing is done. All the plans that one ought to be able to make are simply castles in the air. We can say reasonably definitely that we will get married in August or September, that we will have sixty days leave (such perfect days they will be), then we'll come out to Palestine and that we'll have about two years here before going home again. That's a fairly safe assumption.

That does not stop him building those castles in the air and some of his plans will indeed come to fruition. And yet assumptions and expectations are regularly disrupted by unexpected opportunities.

5th June 1946

I have got to make a most important decision in the next week. They have started a two-year course in Engineering Science at Cambridge. It means two years damned hard work to get an honours degree – it does mean 5/- a day for ever afterwards. It does mean that if I have to leave the army at 45 or so I have a real qualification for a good job. It means living two years in very pleasant surroundings, living with you and our life almost entirely our own. A big decision, but the thing that annoys me is that I <u>cannot</u> talk it over

> with you. It's coming up again and again things to plan and for which, if we are to share life properly, you must have your say.

In fact, he never mentions this opportunity again, and I must assume that he chose not to pursue the application. Once again, I am beguiled by the thought of what might have been. What would my conventional father have made of post-war university life at Cambridge? Would it have helped him challenge the orthodoxy of the officer class of which he was a paid-up member? It was a science course and he would have rubbed shoulders with more intellectual and less conventional men and women. He had a fine mind and with a science degree he could have taken a very different career path, one that might have opened his intellect in a way that the military career he does pursue would never encourage. And as for my mother, might she have signed up for a course that would have stretched her mind in ways that were never on offer during her time as an 'army wife'?

Throughout his life he had an interest in languages and had taken lessons in Italian and German in the POW camp. He was an enthusiastic communicator and as he believed that he was going to be stuck in the Middle East for some time, it would be wise to be able to speak to the 'natives'.

> I had my first lesson in Arabic this evening and got on like a house of fire. It is great fun. I learnt how to spell your name. This is Pam in Arabic .. دات بپ ام Rather nice isn't it. You start from left to right and there isn't a P in Arabic so they designed

> *a special symbol for you!*

As the wedding approaches there is more communication about how to reconcile his mother to the fact that she is indeed 'losing' her son. Pam's mother has been doing her best to pour oil on troubled waters.

> 18th June 1946
>
> *Your ma wrote me a sweet letter about the weekend with my mama, and said the same as you: charming but a little overwrought on the subject of you and I. Her advice was to keep my mouth shut and let her find herself in a whirl, so that she didn't necessarily think about it too much. Oh, darling I'd have given anything for this not to have happened, still it can't be helped so we might as well accept it.*

The phrase "a little overwrought" seems to be doing a lot of work there.

As he could have predicted, the Jewish resistance is hotting up and is bound to have an impact on the chances of Pam joining him in Palestine.

> 20th June
>
> *It looks awfully as if the war is about to start out here,*

again. There is a lot of nonsense going on: blowing bridges, terrorism etc. I am glad in one way, as I want it over before you arrive, so that we can enjoy Palestine and not for ever wondering if you are alright. But with all this kidnapping and general nonsense I'd loath to be caught out by these damned Yehedis.

As we have seen, a month later the British presence in Palestine is indeed 'caught out' by the Haganah, or to be more precise, its most radical wing the Irgun who were responsible for the bombing of the King David Hotel in Jerusalem on the 22nd July 1946. A day later Drew writes:

The "King David" do is a proper nasty show. We haven't had the official casualties – the place is in a shambles with people working 24 hours a day to get the bodies out. In one way, although it is beastly to say it, it puts the Yehedis completely out of court and we can, I think do almost anything to them now. They have completely lost any world approval and it will certainly lower their stock in the States. But reverting from the politics, darling, I don't think it is going to interfere with our plans. It had better not!

His reference to the loss of 'world approval' has a powerful echo in the global response to the current Israeli government's systematic destruction of Gaza and annihilation of so many of the Palestinians who live there. Whilst I would repudiate his assumption that British troops could do "almost anything to them now" as well as the anti-Semitic tone of some of his rhetoric, I can empathise with his frustration.

Later in the same letter he addresses what must seem like a more pressing issue: Pam has suggested that he wear morning coat for the wedding and that this could be hired for the occasion.

> *Don't worry about Moss Bros. I am going to wear uniform! My batman has been polishing up the boots and is in at the moment organising my breeches and my Sam Brown. Roger is lending me his sword. So, there we are, fully dressed without reverting to the Brothers Moss.*

The wedding has been fixed for early in September. It seems the army is more accommodating when it comes to leave to get married. With one month to go, Drew is counting the days

3rd August

> *This a busy letter. There is so much to do, so quickly, handing over to everybody here but above all our private affairs. My darling heart it is so little time now. Soon I'll hear your voice and then actually see you. I don't want a preview of the wedding dress, I want to see it as it should be worn, on the day, in church.*

A week later he has started his journey home and he is in Cairo waiting to travel to Port Said to board the ship that will carry him home.

8th August

I am sitting on the verandah watching the lights of Cairo across the Nile and I am feeling very you-sick. It is so beautiful and something that ought to be shared with you.

And yet even in the excitement of the impending nuptials he still needs to assuage his reluctant mother and her ambivalence about the whole thing.

I said meet me in London on the 23rd, I think darling, make it the 26th. I must stay three days, at least, at home – to soothe mama. Oh darling, this soothing is so damned unnecessary. I want to rush straight up to London and see you, without waiting for three days at home. But I suppose it may pay dividends later.

I have no idea whether those three days helped overcome his mother's disapproval, but I do know the wedding went ahead with or without her blessing.

The Wedding

Drew Bethell and Pam Woosnam were married on September 7th 1946, in St Mary's Church, Builth Wells, Breconshire. There were over one hundred guests. Among the attendees were Pam's parents who were delighted with the match, and Mrs Kay Bethell who was less so.

1946

The Honeymoon

Pam and Drew spent three weeks on their honeymoon in Sweden. First just outside Stockholm where they stayed at the luxurious Hotellvägen in Saltsjöbadenand, then on the island of Ingaro, 25 miles south of the city. Finally, they spent a few days sailing with friend Nils and Lillemore Tilgren on the island of Härsö.

The wedding and honeymoon seem to have gone very well, but all good things must come an end. The next letter I have is written on the return journey to Palestine. He is flying back. It is his first time in an aeroplane.

> 20th October 1946
> (addressed to Mrs Andrew Bethell!)
>
> Darling heart of mine.
>
> This is a bloody game. Leaving you. I hardly dared to speak when I left you in case I burst into tears. The taxi arrived on time but the twenty-minute journey from you to the aerodrome was one of the longest in my life. After that it wasn't so bad as everything was something new: the plane, the equipment, the engines starting up, taxing out to the runway then we were up and off. All so quick. I looked down and Swindon was miles away and below in a haze. It was ten to eight and I imagined you my sweetheart and what you were doing, not a good occupation, at the moment, it hurts too much.

Once back with his regiment, reality bites:

> 26th October 1946
>
> It's a bit hard this incredible rush back – straight into things, not even a weekend to sort myself out and then supposed to be ready to take the Battery to Transjordan for a month.

Tonight, lying in bed, alone, how the memories and thoughts of you are going to come – how my arm isn't behind your head with the softness of your hair against my cheek. It's no good darling, the only thing to do is to work like hell pulling every string until you are here to share the beastliness that is Palestine now.

A week later the regiment is in Transjordan with the rest of 1st Division. They are engaged in training and exercises. He is living in a tent and finding it hard to cope with yet more separation from his newly wed wife.

1st November 1946

We have been married just eight weeks. Seven of those weeks were the happiest, and then followed by one of the most miserable weeks of my life. Oh, darling it doesn't seem to get any better.

Despite his misery at being separated yet again, he is still a soldier at heart, and once settled in Transjordan his regiment is taking part in a full-scale exercise with the entire Division and it reminds him of the war he left behind in Europe.

This morning as we moved off there was a wonderful picture of "war", just before dawn in a half light. The long columns of infantry plodding slowly forward past a row of tanks with their engines ticking over. The tanks seemed to tower over us blocking the light. The dust was slowly rising and made the whole scene like a dream of things that had happened before. I must say it is odd to be sitting here writing and thinking of you with all the paraphernalia of war around me.

Then after a fourteen-hour day of action he is lying in the open with his sheepskin jacket and one blanket. He only has his military helmet for a pillow as his thoughts return to his new wife:

I started to play the game of "where was I eleven weeks ago". The comparison between the helmet under my head and your breast my darling is too hard to be pleasant.

I treasure this image of the contrast between helmet and breast. It seems to encapsulate the bifurcation of his and my masculinity: soft and hard, sensitive and robust, love and war.

Although he is preoccupied with how and when he will get Pam out to Palestine, he finds time to order up some 'his and hers' reading matter.

11th November

I have ordered from Hatchards, darling, two books. One for you called "Bed Manners". I am told that it is extraordinarily amusing – all the do's and don'ts of the bedroom! They coin such happy phrases as "pillow pal" and "mattress mate". The other book is a new life of Wellington for me.

A few days later he has heard about his book order.

November 27th

I have had a letter from Hatchards saying that "Bed Manners" is being reprinted so I am ordering a copy for us. Your bedroom manners are impeccable. The only thing a carping husband might take exception to is an inability to take anyone or anything seriously in the early morning! My friend Teddy has read it and says it is illuminating and amusing!! It is important not to share the copy with anyone here. It would make discipline very hard if my fellow officers knew that you don't like the way I step out of my clothes!

In the first week of December his optimism about the chances of Pam joining him after Christmas are shattered. All provision for wives has been cancelled due to the continued unrest with the regiment having to remain on a war footing. It feels like the final blow in an ongoing litany of on-again off-again arrangements that have dogged their relationship. Managing the emotional fall out of these vicissitudes is made all the harder by the time-lag between letters.

December 4th 1945

Ever since we fell in love, darling we seem to have spent such aeons of time waiting for each other – or something to happen. And staggering from one week to the next always waiting for news of leave, of

> *quarters or your arrival. The pity is that we cannot share the news other than once a every few days and by the time the answer comes, something else has happened which changes everything. That was the blow of getting your so happy letter about coming in January on the same day that the hammer fell.*

As Christmas approaches, he is hoping for other news: there has been talk of regular soldiers being released to return to jobs in the UK. He has again been 'pulling strings' and thinks he may be on that list.

> *Still no news. Oh, darling how used you must have got to those words. I must say I thought the answer would arrive last night. I felt psychic.*

Sadly, his psychic powers appear to have failed him. It causes him to brood on the downside of the career he has chosen.

> *Regimental soldiering is heart-breaking in a lot of ways. Where the eternal chopping and changing from camp to camp - rushing out to deal with railways, roads and illegals, while not so much wearing as unsettling. I suppose it is a reaction after the intensity of the war.*

I worry that he may have chosen his career whilst still beguiled by that same intensity of war. He cannot have been alone in finding the transition from five years of wartime to peacetime a troublesome business. The word "unsettling' may not be the half of it. But I am delighted to say that on this day his gloom will be short-lived

He has taken a break from writing the letter to go to the Officers Mess. There he finds that, even though he was a day early in his prediction, he was indeed psychic.

> <u>DARLING IT'S COME</u> – *I'm coming HOME! To you my darling. I went to the Mess and there was the C.O. speechless with rage!!! We had a glorious row on the spot, but he can't stop me and I am on my way.*
>
> *I think that I'll have to stay over Christmas, but it will be such a happy Christmas for us both in the sure knowledge that I am coming home. I'll leave here on the 27th and God willing I'll be with you in the first half of January.*
>
> *Oh, darling my so lovely wife. I don't know what to do or what to say. I am so, so pleased with life, to have my darling wife in my arms again. In just three weeks. Oh, my sweet it doesn't matter a damn where we go or what we do – it's <u>us</u> not you and <u>I</u>.*
>
> *Bless you my precious, only twenty-one days at the <u>most</u>. My heart, my love, <u>my wife, I love you.</u>*
>
> *Your so adoring and so happy husband,*
>
> *Drew.*

I have one letter left. It is short and he briefly mentions how hard it has been to leave his comrades: however disgruntled and relieved to be going, these are still some men with whom he has been through four years of hardship and endeavour.

I must say that up until this morning, I was miserable leaving, but now it's over, there is a wonderful feeling of relief. and now the only thing that matters is that I will be with you in less than a fortnight. Darling, darling, I love you.

The 'less than a fortnight was optimistic. He had to wait for a ship and eventually left Port Said in early January. I cannot be precise because I have run out of letters. He is no longer writing to his wife: he is living with her.

What I do know is that just a few days after he arrived back in England, fresh from the heat of the desert, the weather turned. On the 21st of January 1947 there was a heavy snow fall across the country. It was the start of the coldest and longest winter since 1850. The freezing conditions did not let up for two months. Snow drifts blocked roads and public transport was at a standstill. Wartime rationing was still in place but shortages were compounded by the impossibility for growers to harvest or ship produce. There were regular power cuts and solid fuel was in short supply.

These were the conditions in which Pam and Drew began their married life. They moved into Cricket Green Cottage in the first week of February. I imagine there was very little heating.

Their double bed must have been the warmest place to be. Not surprisingly perhaps, I was conceived in the middle of February, (exactly two years since they first met by the Cedars of Lebanon). I was born nine months later on November 17th 1947.

Stoke Newington, London December 2024

Dear Dad,

I am bereft. I have spent the last month reading through your letters. More than a hundred of them. And I have had your voice in my head. For much of the time it was not a voice I recognised. It was the voice of a young man: in love. Your writing was fuelled by passion and longing and I never saw that side of you. I knew there was a romantic side but I rarely witnessed it. Not altogether surprising as you sent me off to boarding school aged seven. I was not around much to see you expressing your love for my mother. Even if I had been, I am pretty sure you would not have wanted to reveal that side of yourself to me and my brother. And it is that expectation of reticence that made my time with this younger version of you so very surprising and joyful.

It was not all lovey-dovey, I also got a glimpse of the older man. There were many traits that I did recognise: your sense of obligation both to your profession and to your friends and family. Your enthusiasm for everything you engaged with: sport, shopping, parties and driving across the desert at dangerous speeds. I could see the mature man, the man who made a success of his career and who was comfortable with the life and role of a soldier. I had cause to compare you in your early twenties with myself and with my children at the same age. It was clear that you had grown up a lot faster than we did. The war must have done that as it did for so many of your fellow warriors. On the other hand, I also think that your generation were much quicker than we were to take on the characteristics of your elders. You sound like a grown up. You are familiar with the routines and the trappings of your class. You shop for hand-made suits, you are confident ordering exotic meals and fine wines in exclusive hotels, you are self-assured in your right to get angry and make demands on others. And yet these things are indeed trappings. When it comes to your emotional life, you are far less secure. There is a naïveté about your approach to sex: you are shocked by the brazen carnality of some of your friends. You are passionate in love, and yet you are threatened by your mother's disapproval.

But this journey is almost over. I have discovered so much of what happened to you in the years before I arrived. And when I ran out of facts, I enjoyed making it up. It was so satisfying to pretend I was with you on the beaches of Dunkirk, on the side of Recce Ridge, on the Beach Head at Anzio and steep slopes of Monte Grande. I will never know how close I got to your lived experience, but I would want you to admire my efforts. I have certainly emerged with a greater understanding of what made you the man you were. When I tried to start the process of getting to know you better in the Pizzeria you were not having it. I like to think if you had been able to read this book, you might have opened up a little more. Break the habit of your lifetime and the lifetimes of so many of your generation and accepted my best intentions.

This is where I step back. I was always going to stop once I was in the picture. However, I owe it to my readers and to you, to record what you did with the rest of your life. It was impressive. So, I am adding your obituary as it appeared in your regimental journal.

Of course, it is all too late and it breaks my heart that I cannot give this book to you. You have been absent for so long, but I finish this journey with so much belated, but heartfelt love.

Hum

OBITUARY

MAJOR-GENERAL D.A.D.J. BETHELL
6th February 1921 — 6th February 1988

By Major-General M.J. Tomlinson, CB,

Drew Bethell was born in Dar es Salaam in 1921 and was educated at Sherborne. He joined the Royal Military Academy with a Kitchener Scholarship in August 1939. On the outbreak of war, he was quickly diverted to an OCTU and was commissioned into the Regiment in February 1940. He served with 19th Field Regiment until March 1943. As an OP officer in Tunisia, in support of 4th Battalion Grenadier Guards, he volunteered to join the 1st Battalion Irish Guards for their attack on Recce Ridge at Medjez-el-Bab. This attack, to prevent the Germans reinforcing their lines, was of an intensity that from No 2 Company and their OP party only six men returned. The remainder were killed or wounded. Drew was wounded and captured. His hearing was thereafter impaired for the rest of his life. It eventually took two full divisional attacks to secure Recce Ridge.

Drew was taken to a Prisoner of War Camp in Northern Italy. He escaped and walked some 450 miles along the Apennine mountains to the Allied Lines in Southern Italy. He eventually rejoined 19th Regiment and continued to serve with them until 1947. Drew served in 3rd Regiment for a short spell before going to Staff College in 1950. After a tour as BMRA in 11th Armoured Division he joined 2nd Regiment in 1953 then to serve on the staff in Canada for three years from 1955. In 1959 he joined 1st Regiment to command The Chestnut Troop. He undertook this as he did most things with pride, exacting standards and a caring detachment that was the hallmark of his performance. He had great style and many friends, but something in him would never let them get too close. As a young officer in Hohne for much of the 1950s I saw a great deal of Pam and Drew. They were generous, friendly and always had time for the young.

After a tour as an Instructor at the Staff College, Drew took command of 26th Field Regiment in Malaya. The Regiment supported the Commonwealth Brigade and had its own integral Australian Field Battery. Drew was respected and well-liked by the affiliated, experienced and tough Australian and New Zealand Battalions. The judgement of his CRA, at the time, was that his Regiment received high acclaim for its operational ability in the many facets of Jungle Warfare. Once again Pam and Drew were generous and charming in their hospitality to the endless procession of Commonwealth guests.

Drew brought his Regiment home to Shoeburyness and almost at once took them, at notice of but a few days, to undertake an emergency tour, playing a key role, with the United Nations Force Cyprus in the early days of the troubles in 1962. I was by then one of his Battery Commanders. Anyone could talk absolutely straight to Drew Bethell and he would talk straight right back. If you could convince him he would accept the argument but if you did not, he would see you off in a quite dramatic way. He was a straight man. Throughout his latter service Drew remained utterly consistent. He set his own priorities based on his own judgement. If these did not coincide with the views of others, he would listen to them, but if unconvinced, he would not change. He had a remarkable gift of getting his own way, with a charming smile.

He rationalised and revitalised the artillery support for the 3rd Division when he was CRA. He returned to Canada again to attend the National Defence College and lived and enjoyed every minute of the experience. By the time he was

Deputy Commandant of the Staff College his single-minded, and relatively lately acquired, enthusiasm for sailing, had reached what some of his friends would suggest had become near obsession. An active member of the Royal Artillery Yacht Club and the Royal Cruising Club he was also an accomplished fisherman, a fine shot and an energetic golfer. He completed his service as a practical and astute President of the Regular Commissions Board. He was good with the young, they listened to him, and he listened to them. His Warrant Officers respected him, loved him but were wary of him. They did not always understand him, but many stories about him have been told and retold in Sergeants' Messes over the years.

My own service made contact with Drew during six of his eleven appointments from 1951. He was always my friend but I never felt that I knew him really well. I enjoyed serving under him, and with him for if you met his high standards he regarded subordinates as serving with him, but he was always 'The Boss'. That was his way.

Since retirement he had been a capable and caring Warden of Sackville College, a 17th Century Alms-house, housing eighteen elderly residents. He remained an avid sailor navigating the seas singlehanded. He would quickly involve himself with fellow sailors, fishermen, locals of all varieties, in four different languages. Always hospitable, always a glass of something to be had on his boat. To the end, a devoted family man, it is to Pam and Andrew that thoughts must turn. Drew was a professional Gunner of significant style and held in considerable affection by those who served with him. He left the Regiment a better and worthier place for his service. A member of No 2 Company 1st Battalion Irish Guards in 1943 was at his Memorial Service. Such was the man. He will be missed.

SOURCES

When my father died there was no such thing as Google and although it took me longer than I would have liked to get around to writing this book, the delay has meant I have been blessed with the power of internet search and even in some cases with AI. However, I have also made use of several key texts to provide the background to my father's story.

For his experience on the beach of Dunkirk I read first-hand accounts many of which came from the BBC's *History Archive: the Voices of Dunkirk*. I also read *Dunkirk :Nine Days That Saved an Army* by John Grehan.

For the Battle of Recce Ridge, I used the first-hand accounts from the regimental records of the Irish Guards.

Life in and escape from Camp PG49 has been covered by several writers. *Love and War in the Apennines* by Eric Newby, *The Pebble in the Skull* by Stuart Hood and most recently in *Where the Hell Have You Been* by Tom Carver.

In describing the Italian campaign from Anzio to Monte Grande I was guided along the way by A.M. Cheetham who was a young artillery officer in the companion regiment to my father's part of 1st Division. His book *Ubique* provided me with so much of the detail, particularly of the role of FOO, that helped me recreate my father's experience. I was also lucky to find at the Imperial War Museum the papers of the Commanding Officer of 19th Field Regiment, Colonel R.B. Grieg, which included a detailed account of the regiment's time on the Anzio beach head. The IWM also found me a rare copy of *History of the First Division: Florence to Monte Grande:* an official history gathered from senior staff.

The background to my father's time in Palestine largely came from *'A Senseless and Squalid War' Voices from Palestine 1945-1948* by Norman Rose.

To watch the film The Stranger at the Gate go to:
www.tricornerbooks.co.uk

ACKNOWLEDGEMENTS

This book could not have happened without the help of Sylvia Spalding who found the relevant regimental records in the National Archives with research skills well beyond mine. I was also lucky to have contacted Gerard Wood at the Gibraltar National Archives who found the cuttings about my grandfather which proved invaluable in piecing together the picture of his suicide. Rachel Hassell, the admirable archivist at Sherborne School was generous with her time and found all the contemporary references to my father which added so much to my account of his life at school.

Several friends have read drafts of this book and given me the encouragement to persevere. Marion Stevenson has been a constant source of positive and perceptive feedback. Sandy Balfour and Michael Simons offered valuable suggestions. Paul Ashton has applied his forensic eye to my errant prose.

Finally, Rosemary Davies gave me the caring help and support I needed to keep me going, whilst adding her analytic insight to the emotional journey taken by my father and myself.

ANDREW BETHELL

After a year teaching at a Canadian boarding school, Andrew spent the next seventeen in Inner London comprehensives, where he helped pioneer media studies as a curriculum subject, wrote and edited a series of play-scripts and media studies textbooks. In 1987 he set up Double Exposure, a television production company which went on to make a wide range of documentaries and educational series, many of which won awards and large audiences in the UK and US. In 1997 he won the BAFTA for best documentary series for The House, a six-part series that went behind the scenes at the Royal Opera House to much acclaim and controversy. He was the CEO and Creative Director of Teachers TV, a television channel for teachers and parents and in 2011 he went to San Francisco to set up Teaching Channel, which runs to this day. He is an active chair of governors for several primary schools and lives in North London.

Also by
ANDREW BETHELL

Dearest Brother

A MEMOIR OF SUICIDE AND SIBLING RIVALRY

Forty years ago, my brother killed himself. At the time I played the part of a grieving brother, but it was a sham. Just beneath the surface there was a pulse of anger, fed by a sense of guilt which corrupted my memories of him and diminished the last of brotherly love. It may be late in the day but now I am determined to re-discover my love for the brother I lost and perhaps understand why he ended his life.

Dearest Brother is a gripping account of that journey of discovery: from a post war childhood, to a boarding school education on to Western Australia and the New Age world of the sixties.

An excellent book: wonderfully well written., honest and extremely wise.
Nick Luxmoore Author: 'Young People, Death and the unfairness of Everything'

An extraordinary story, brilliantly told. Blake saw the world in a grain of sand; Bethell finds it in his quest to know his brother.
Sandy Balfour Author 'Vulnerable in Hearts: A Memoir of Fathers, Sons and Contract Bridge'

Available from
- amazon.co.uk
- waterstones.com
- barnesandnoble.com

www.ingramcontent.com/pod-product-compliance
Lightning Source LLC
Chambersburg PA
CBHW020355080526
44584CB00014B/1031